THE SAINT NICHOLAS LITURGY

THE SAINT NICHOLAS LITURGY

And Its Literary Relationships
(*Ninth to Twelfth Centuries*)

By Charles W. Jones

With an Essay on the Music
By Gilbert Reaney

UNIVERSITY OF CALIFORNIA PRESS
BERKELEY AND LOS ANGELES
1963

UNIVERSITY OF CALIFORNIA PUBLICATIONS
ENGLISH STUDIES: 27

ADVISORY EDITORS: H. G. DICK, J. J. ESPEY, WILLIAM FROST,
C. W. JONES, M. R. PROCTOR, H. N. SMITH, LINDA VAN NORDEN

Approved for publication November 2, 1962
Issued October 25, 1963
Price, $3.50

UNIVERSITY OF CALIFORNIA PRESS
BERKELEY AND LOS ANGELES
CALIFORNIA

◇

CAMBRIDGE UNIVERSITY PRESS
LONDON, ENGLAND

© 1963 BY THE REGENTS OF THE UNIVERSITY OF CALIFORNIA
PRINTED IN THE UNITED STATES OF AMERICA

ACKNOWLEDGMENT

ALTHOUGH IT IS IMPOSSIBLE to acknowledge the generous help of many colleagues and librarians both at home and abroad, I do wish especially to thank Professor Robert Palmer of Pomona College, whose comments and corrections were invaluable, and Professor Gilbert Reaney of the University of California, Los Angeles, who prepared the appended musicological essay.

C. W. J.

CONTENTS

Bibliographic Abbreviations ix

   I. Introduction 1

  II. The Nero Manuscript 7

 III. The Text 14

 IV. Relevant Legends of Nicholas 42

   V. Legends About the Liturgy 47

 VI. Authorship of the Liturgy 63

VII. Otloh's *Vita S. Nicolai* 74

VIII. The Miracle Plays 90

 IX. Conclusion 118

Appendix A. Decasyllabic Verse of the Hildesheim Plays . 122

Appendix B. The Music of the St. Nicholas Liturgy,

   by Gilbert Reaney 140

Bibliographic Abbreviations

Aberdeen Breviary [William Blew, editor] *Breviarium Aberdonense*. London, For the Bannatyne Club, 1854. 2 vols.

Acta SS Socii Bollandiani. *Acta Sanctorum*. [Begun by J. Bollandus.] Antwerp and Brussels, 1643–

Albrecht Otto Albrecht. *Four Latin Plays of St. Nicholas*. Philadelphia, Univ. of Pa. Press, 1935.

Anal. Boll. Socii Bollandiani. *Analecta Bollandiana*. Brussels, 1882–

Anal. Hymn. C. Blume and G. M. Dreves, eds. *Analecta Hymnica Medii Aevi*. Leipzig, 1886–1922. 55 vols.

Anrich Gustav Anrich. *Hagios Nikolaos*. Leipzig, 1913–1917. 2 vols.

Auda Antoine Auda. *Étienne de Liège*. Liège, 1923.

BHL Socii Bollandiani. *Bibliotheca Hagiographica Latina* (Subsidia Hagiographica, No. 6). Brussels, 1900–1901. 2 vols.

Cat. Cod. Brux. Socii Bollandiani. *Catalogus Codicum Hagiographicorum Bibliothecae Regiae Bruxellensis*. Brussels, 1886–1889. 3 vols.

Cat. Cod. Paris. Socii Bollandiani. *Catalogus Codicum Hagiographicorum Latinorum in B. N. Parisiensi*. Brussels, 1890. 3 vols.

Chevalier, *Bayeux* Ulysse Chevalier. *Ordinaire et coutumier de Bayeux (xiiie siècle)* (Bibliothèque Liturgique VIII^2). Paris, 1902.

Chevalier, *Laon* Ulysse Chevalier. *Ordinaires de l'église cathédrale de Laon* (Bibliothèque Liturgique VI). Paris, 1897.

Chevalier, *Repert.* Ulysse Chevalier. *Repertorium Hymnologicum*. Louvain, 1892–1921. 6 vols.

Coffman, *Craig* *Renaissance Studies in Honor of Hardin Craig*. Stanford, 1941.

Coffman, *Manly* See *Manly*.

Coffman, *New Theory* George R. Coffman. *A New Theory Concerning the Origin of the Miracle Play* (Diss., Univ. of Chicago). Menasha, Wis., 1914.

Collette A. Collette. *Histoire de bréviaire de Rouen*. Rouen, 1902.

DACL Don Fernand Cabrol and Dom Henri Leclercq, eds. *Dictionnaire d'archéologie chrétienne et de liturgie*. Paris, 1907–

Darlington Reginald R. Darlington, *The* Vita Wulfstani *of William of Malmesbury* (Camden Third Series, XL). London, Royal Historical Society, 1928.

Du Méril, *Poésies* Edelstand Du Méril. *Poésies populaires latines antérieures au xiie siécle*. Paris, 1843.

Falconius Nicholas Carminius Falconius. *Sancti Confessoris Pontificis ... Nicolai Acta Primigenia,* Naples, 1751.

Fliche et Martin   *Histoire de l'Église,* fondée par Augustin Fliche et Victor Martin, Paris, 1935–   18 vols. [to be complete in 24 vols.]

HBSP   *Henry Bradshaw Society Publications.* London, 1888–

Hanssens   J. M. Hanssens, ed. *Amalarii Episcopi Opera Liturgica Omnia.* Rome, Studi e testi, 1950. 3 vols.

John   John the Deacon, of Naples, *Vita Sancti Nicholai.* [For editions, see Falconius; Mombritius.]

Knowles   David Knowles. *The Monastic Order in England.* Cambridge, 1950.

Kurth   Godefroid Kurth. *Notger de Liège.* Brussels, 1905. 2 vols.

Leroquais, *Brév.*   Abbé V. Leroquais. *Les bréviaires manuscripts des bibliothéques publiques de France.* Paris, 1934. 5 vols.

Mon. Germ. Hist.   G. H. Pertz, Th. Mommsen, and others, eds. Monumenta Germaniae Historica. [In titled sections.] Folio series, Berlin, 1826–1896: Quarto series, Berlin, 1876–

Manitius   Max Manitius, *Geschichte der lateinischen Literatur des Mittelalters* (Müller's Handbuch der klassischen Altertumswissenschaft, IX). Munich, 1911–1931. 3 vols.

Manly   *The Manly Anniversary Studies.* Chicago, 1923.

Meisen   Karl Meisen. *Nikolauskult und Nikolausbrauch im Abendlande* (Forschungen zur Volkskunde, Heft 9–12). Düsseldorf, 1931.

Meyer, *Ges. Abh.*   Wilhelm Meyer. *Gesammelte Abhandlungen zur mittellateinischen Rhythmik.* Berlin, 1905–1936. 3 vols.

Mombritius   Bonino Mombrizio. *Sanctuarium seu vitae sanctorum.* Solesmes and Paris, 1910. 2 vols. [Originally published at Milan before 1480.]

Mone   F. J. Mone, *Lateinische Hymnen des Mittelalters.* Freiburg, 1853–1855. 3 vols.

Ordinale Exon.   J. N. Dalton, ed. *Ordinale Exon.* (*HBSP* XXXVII, XXXVIII, LXIII, LXXIX). 1909–1940. 4 vols.

Pat. Lat.   J. P. Migne. *Patrologia Latina Cursus Completus.* Paris, 1844–1864. 221 vols.

Pietzsch   Gerhard Pietzsch. *Studien zur Geschichte der Musiktheorie im Mittelalter.* Halle, 1932. 2 vols.

Pitra   Cardinal J. B. Pitra. *Analecta Sacra* (Spicilegium Solesmense), *Parata I.* Paris, 1876.

Portiforium   Anselm Hughes, ed. *The Portiforium of St. Wulstan* (*HBSP,* XC). London, 1960.

Young, *Drama*   Karl Young. *The Drama of the Medieval Church.* Oxford, 1933. 2 vols.

Young, *Manly*   See *Manly.*

Chapter I

Introduction

The *Oxford Dictionary of the Christian Church*[1] briefly summarizes the common knowledge of the cult of Nicholas:

Nicholas, St., Bp. of Myra in Lycia. Though one of the most popular saints in both the Greek and Latin Churches, scarcely anything is historically certain about him. Acc. to tradition, he was imprisoned during the Diocletianic persecution and afterwards released, and was present at the Council of Nicea. The latter supposition is most improbable as he is not in any of the early lists of bishops present at the Council, nor referred to in the writings of Athanasius. He is first definitely met with in the Church of 'St. Priscus and St. Nicholas', built by the Emp. Justinian (d. 565) at Constantinople. His cult became popular in the W. after the inhabitants of Bari claimed to have got possession of his remains on 9 May 1087.

St. Nicholas is regarded as the patron saint of sailors, and churches under his dedication are often built so that they could be seen off the coast as landmarks. He is also the patron saint of children, bringing them gifts on 6 Dec. (whence 'Santa Claus', an American corruption of 'Saint Nicholas'). And he is also the patron saint of Russia. His symbol is sometimes three bags of gold, the dowry he is supposed to have given to three girls to save them from degradation, sometimes three children standing in a tub at his side, a representation which has been variously explained. Feast Day, 6 Dec.

As reserved a scholar as Karl Young quoted approvingly the long-standing phrase, "most popular saint in Christendom." This popularity,[2] especially in a Middle Age given to hagiolatry,

---

[1] F. L. Cross, ed., Oxford, 1958, p. 954.

[2] Anrich edited the Byzantine texts. Because of the scarcity of copies of this valuable work, I have not been able to consult it as regularly as I have wished. Anrich traced the development of the Greek-Byzantine cult; cf. II, p. 441. Max Herzog zu Sachsen, *Das christliche Hellas*, Leipzig, 1918, pp. 324–326, states that of 4,637 churches in the Greek world, 752 are dedicated to the Virgin (inc. 282 Dormition), 189 to John the Baptist, 75 to the prophet Elias, 43 to Theodore, 193 to Athanasius, 291 to George, 69 to Constantine, 165 to Parasceve (*Bibliotheca Hagiographica Graeca*, No. 1420), and 359 to Nicholas. M. G. Schlumberger, "Les sceux Byzantins," *Memoires de la Soc. des Antiquaires de France*, XLIV (1883), pp. 9–10, reported that Nicholas' image

has made the mastery of all available evidence of cult a superhuman task. Nicholas was patron not only of nations, cities, towns, and villages, but of guilds and confreries and orders, and of virtually every vocation, religious and secular, urban and rural. Though the impact of the Nicholas cult upon the various medieval arts is obvious, that impact has not been calculated with precision.[3] Each historian's conclusions are accurate only within the limitations he has set for himself.

Because many of the histories have centered upon the exciting theft of Nicholas' relics from Myra and the Translation to Norman Bari, in Aquileia, in 1087—one of the most journalistic actions of the Middle Ages—it is customary to think of the western cult as a product of that event. But it may be possible that the Translation was the result of growing popularity, rather than the cause. The graph of pilgrimage and tourism to the east ascends sharply throughout the eleventh century.[4] Count Fulk Nerra of Anjou, "the Jerusalem traveler," who began a cult of Nicholas at Angers around 1020,[5] may have been only one and not the earliest of many cultists in the Latin west. The cults of Catherine of Constantinople and of the friends of Jesus (Lazarus, Magdalen), equally oriental, spread through the

---

is second only to that of the Virgin. Nicholas joins Basil, John Chrysostom, and Gregory Nazianzus in the tetrarchy of bishop saints; see Charles Diehl, *Manuel d'art byzantin*, II, 1926, p. 511. On the churches in Constantinople, see R. Janin in *Echoes d'orient* (Oct.–Dec. 1932), pp. 408–410. Although this is not the place to consider his popularity in the West, I call attention that Frances Arnold-Foster, *Studies in Church-Dedications*, 3 vols., London, 1899, gives these numbers for pre-Reformation England: Andrew 577, Nicholas 385, Margaret 230, Lawrence 220, George 202, Martin 151, Helena 113, Thomas of Canterbury 69, Cuthbert 65, Gregory the Great 28. Huelson's census lists 25 Nicholas-dedications in the city of Rome. Chevalier's *Repert.* lists 284 hymns and sacred poems for Nicholas as compared with 266 for Martin; the other comparable saints are Agnes, Augustine, Barbara, Benedict, Catherine, and Ursala.

[3] The Bollandists' *Acta Sanctorum* has not yet reached 6 December. The most comprehensive treatment is that of Karl Meisen, *Nikolauskult und Nikolausbrauch im Abendlande*. Meisen was primarily concerned with codifying the evidences of beginnings of modern folk customs. For patronage, consult his Index, *s.v.* "Patronate des hl. N."

[4] R. W. Southern, *Making of the Middle Ages*, 1953, pp. 51–53. "The civilization of the twelfth century owes a great deal to the tears which were shed in the eleventh."

[5] On his founding of Saint-Nicolas-d'Angers, see the Bollandists' *Catalogus Codicum Hagiographicorum Latinorum in B. N. Parisiensi*, III (Brussels, 1890), pp. 158–162.

Introduction 3

west in the eleventh century.⁶ Alphanus of Salerno, who died two years before the Translation, composed hymns to Nicholas, possibly as early as 1055, in one of which he maintained that Rome regarded Nicholas as the equal of the Apostles:

> Te mirabiliter colit
> Laudat, magnificat Graecia nobilis,
> Immo totius orbis haec
> Gaudet meta tibi munera solvere.
> Mundi Roma caput suis
> Aequalem celebrat semper apostolis,
> Cujus crebra juvamina
> Non multis precibus quaerit et impetrat.⁷

To be sure, Alphanus was cisalpine; but the Holy Empire was in flower, and sentiments would only slightly differ in the Teutonized north.

The image of Nicholas, as it emerged in the west, was more secular than religious. That secularity was present from the beginning. Indeed, the earliest characteristics of Nicholas persist even to this day, however many the superficial changes which came as a result of historical events. For example, recently many psychoanalysts, observing the high incidence of psychic disturbance in December, have tried to study the history of images of Nicholas, Santa Claus, and the like, in the hope that they might find a key to those disturbances.⁸ They have found ample material. Nicholas legends of the late Middle Age, as they appear in the west, repeat themes of murder and demonic possession; they arouse crass sensation, not piety. The rise of the cult was coincident with the rise of trade and the bourgeoisie; but the legends appealed to every class to the extent that it was interested in the sensational rather than spiritual. The more obvious

---

⁶ See [Etienne Michel Faillon], *Monuments inédits sur l'apostolat de sainte Marie-Madeleine en Provence, et sur les autres apôtres de cette contrée, saint Lazare, saint Maximin, sainte Marthe, et les saintes maries Jacobé et Salomé*, 2 vols., Paris, Migne, 1848; Coffman, *New Theory*, pp. 67–68.

⁷ *Analecta Hymn.* XXII (1895), p. 205, No. 348.

⁸ The most recent to come to my attention is that of Dr. Adriaan D. deGroot, *The Myth of St. Nicholas: A Psychoanalytic and Historical Study*, 1962; based on his *Sint Nicolaas, patroon von liefde*, Amsterdam, 1949.

commercial drives, which to this day show no sign of slackening, led ambitious merchants to plan and execute the Translation of relics from Myra to Bari. The Translation grew out of the commercial rivalry between the Norman Barians and the Venetians. Russia and Byzantium might well have been disturbed at a rape analogous to the present-day theft of a Leonardo. Instead, they hailed the deed as a triumph throughout the Christian east. Political expediency has been offered as the reason.[9] Indeed, as stated above, there is no extant evidence that an actual or historical Nicholas ever existed. Yet the strategic location of the port of Myra is in itself evidence enough why an image like that of Nicholas developed there. Men of commerce needed special protection against pirates and other perils of the sea just at that geographical point. Chances are that when, if ever, the available evidence is codified, the most popular saint in Christendom may prove to be the least essentially religious saint of all.

My own curiosity about the cult was aroused in a common fashion. As a student of literature, I wondered why the first medieval secular dramas should have had Nicholas as their subject. Since medieval secular and lay records are tantalizingly few, and there is but slight agreement about how those few are to be interpreted, I have found the most immediate help at that point where the records are most readily available—in the Church. Nicholas did have a life in the Church, though a nebulous one. Among the ecclesiastical records that have survived are many service books, though their survival has been a chance affair, since they were often purposely destroyed. In these books, the Office for St. Nicholas Day has been the most helpful. Despite the accelerated activity of critics, historians, and musicologists recently, no reliable work has directly traced the history of that liturgy. The following pages supply some information about its peregrinations which may more sharply define the effect of a popular image by tracing the spread of the Christian worship that incorporated it.

---

[9] See, e.g., Bernard Leib, *Rome, Kiev, et Byzance,* Paris, 1924, Bk. i, Ch. 3.

Introduction 5

From the middle of the twelfth century to the redesign of the Roman Rite during the counterreformation, Nicholas Day, December 6, is marked in western liturgical calendars by rubrics or other designations indicating a major feast, often with *viii* or *xii lectiones, in cappis,* or the like. Some, indeed, mark an octave,[10] with lessons and anthems extending through the week. After pope Urban II established May 9, the anniversary of the Translation, as a major feast for the diocese of Bari,[11] many northern churches followed suit. Individual hymns, anthems, responses, and proses, and partial collections have been published from time to time; but except for Birch's transcript, mentioned below, the most nearly complete representation of the liturgy is the text which Karl Young reproduced from two French manuscripts: it represents the verbal texts of a monastic cursus for the Day.[12]

To my knowledge, no one has faced the question of how many medieval liturgies existed, though the words of many recent historians suggest that there were several and that the cult drew upon the creative energies of many a provincial composer. This notion is correct for hymns and proses, of which there are many,[13] but not for the cursus. There was never more than one liturgy, though the order of the items was often changed and abridged to conform with local custom.[14] I can offer no specific

---

[10] Leroquais, *Brév.* (consult Index). Leroquais remarks (I, p. lxvi) that it would be very surprising if a convent dedicated to St. Nicholas did not have an octave. I calculate, after adding the instances I know to those of Meisen's census (pp. 126–171), that there were more than 600 cloisters in the medieval Latin world dedicated to St. Nicholas; this figure does not include churches and chapels.

[11] Decree at Bari, A.D. 1089. Mansi, *Concilia,* XX(1775), cols. 645–646.

[12] In *Manly,* pp. 259–263. Both manuscripts were written at the abbey of St. Maur-des-Fossés; they are now Paris B.N. MSS *Latin 12584* (*saec.* xi²), fos. 383ᵛ–385ᵛ, and *12044* (*saec.* xii).

[13] See Chevalier, *Repert.,* VI, pp. 164–65, for a partial and somewhat dated list; cf. Adalbert Ebner, *Quellen und Forschungen z. Gesch. und Kunstgesch. des Missale Romanum im M.A.,* Freiburg i. Br., 1896, pp. 19, 40, 52, 81, 85, 89, 111. Also Leroquais, *Brév.* (consult Index), and E. Misset and W. H. I. Weale, *Thesauris Hymnologicis...* Suppl., Bruges (II, Prosae), 1892, pp. 478–479. Leroquais lists roughly 400 Nicholas items, contained in possibly 350 separate codices, overwhelmingly of *saec.* xiv. As the title indicates, his census was limited to French public libraries.

[14] What were called *epitomata, breviaria itineria,* or *portabilia*—that is, outlines of the office by initia—grew popular from the eleventh century (see Collette, p. 68). Such books, not designed for use in the choir but for private reference, better survived the destruction of the Reformation period.

information regarding the influence of Byzantium on western liturgy of the period, but I hope that the data assembled below may form a basis for future studies.

Although I have not attempted an exhaustive examination of western breviaries, the text which is both the earliest and the most nearly complete, to my knowledge, is that contained in the British Museum MS *Cotton Nero E 1*.[15] I therefore use it as my text. Even though Birch had previously published a transcription, I have edited the whole in order that the subsequent discussion will be properly grounded. The range of my investigation is indicated by my concluding chapter. Establishing the early history of the Office and its position in the cult has been my central purpose, but I have allowed myself latitude for consideration of such literary developments as were entwined with it.

---

[15] I am grateful to Professor Francis Wormald, who first directed my attention to the item.

Chapter II

The Nero Manuscript

NERO E 1 IS A PASSIONALE from Worcester related closely to Cambridge manuscripts *Corpus Christi College* 9 and *C.C.C.* 391 (from Worcester).[1] The Cotton Catalogue of 1802[2] dates the Nero *ca*. A.D. 1000, but Professor Ker sets the date *ca*. 1060.[3] Although Nero (Part II, fos. 153^v–155^v) is the only one of the three related manuscripts to contain the Nicholas liturgy, that liturgy is written in the same hand, or at least in the same kind of ink and format, as the other early sections of the Nero volumes.

It is a complete liturgy, with neumes for the musical portions. Because it is one of only a few liturgies included among otherwise purely hagiographical texts, it has received but slight attention. In 1886, Walter de Gray Birch transcribed the verbal text, together with lections found in British Museum MS *Arundel 91* (*saec*. xii), as an illustration of the legendary life of Nicholas.[4] It is a satisfactorily accurate transcript but is difficult to use, primarily because the transcriber closely followed the capricious

---

[1] The first of these Worcester manuscripts contains, pp. 26–53, John the Deacon's *Vita* with addenda, and inserted leaves of *saec*. xii containing additions to that Life. See M. R. James, *Cat. MSS Corpus Christi College,* I (1909), pp. 21–30, and Parker's catalogue of that collection, 1777, pp. 4, 5. Francis Wormald, *English Kalendars Before A.D. 1100,* I (HBSP LXXII, 1933), pp. 3–14, calls that Corpus manuscript *saec*. xi^1, while affirming its Worcester origin. MS *391* will be discussed below.

[2] P. 239. C. H. Turner, *Early Worcester MSS,* Oxford, 1916, p. lxxi, gives the same date.

[3] Neil Ker, *English Manuscripts in the Century Before the Norman Conquest,* Oxford, 1960, p. 49; cf. p. 53, "seems to have been written a little before the Conquest." Ker also treats the manuscript in *Catalogue of MSS. Containing Anglo-Saxon,* p. 41; *British Museum Quarterly,* XIV (1940), p. 82; and *Medieval Libraries of Great Britain,* pp. 97, 116. On the relation of the two Worcester manuscripts, see Wilhelm Levison in Mon. Germ. Hist., *Script. Rerum Merov.,* VII (Conspectus Codicum Hagiogr.), pp. 545–546.

[4] *Journal of the British Archaeological Association,* XLII, pp. 190–201. The catalogue term *passionale* evidently diverted attention. On the variety of medieval service books and the indefiniteness of accepted terms, see S. J. P. Van Dijk and J. S. Walker, *The Origins of the Modern Roman Liturgy,* 1960, pp. 26–32, etc. "Adequate studies on the medieval terminology of liturgical books are not yet available" (p. 65).

punctuation of the scribe. The Nero text differs from nearly all others which I have examined in that it gives not only all the propers for the Office, including full texts of the lections, but also an outline of the propers for the Mass, including full texts of those propers not elsewhere represented.

The twelve lections differ slightly from those in other manuscripts, even those of the British and Sarum Rites. In Nero they have been selected without any important verbal change from the *Vita Nicolai,* written *ca.* 880 by John, deacon of the abbey of St. January in Naples, which has been printed in several versions.[5] In other manuscripts, the selections from John have in places been abridged or paraphrased, apparently only to attain brevity. Only one, the late manuscript from Hyde Abbey, has included any legend or other matter not directly derived from the earliest and most authentic version of what John wrote.

The Nero manuscript almost certainly was written under the direction of Wulfstan, "the last of the Anglo-Saxon bishops," who was born *ca.* 1012, became bishop in 1062 after years as master and prior, and died in 1092.[6] Although he retained his see after the Conquest while some compatriots were losing theirs, there is no reason to believe that he was a fellow-traveler with the Normans—indeed, in the early years he was involved in some bitter quarrels with them. I know nothing informative about his relations with any part of the Continent.

---

[5] *Bibliotheca Hagiographica Latina* (Subsidia Hagiographica, No. 6), Brussels, 1898–1899, Nos. 6104–6113. Because the Bollandist volume of the *Acta SS* for 6 December has not yet appeared (there is a brief outline of the history of the cult in the *Propylaeum* for December, Brussels, 1940, pp. 568–569), I have had to use rather antiquated editions. My primary text, since it most nearly reflects John's own, is that of Bonino Mombrizio, *Sanctuarium seu vitae sanctorum.* I also use regularly Nicolas Carminius Falconius, *Sancti Confessoris Pontificis...Nicolai Acta Primigenia,* Naples, 1751; John's *Vita,* from Vatican MS *Regin. Lat. 5696,* appears pp. 112 ff. I have also checked Aloysius Lipomanus (bp. of Verona), *De vitis sanctorum,* Louvain, 1568, pp. 252–288, who followed Mombritius, and the *Epitome* (*BHL* Nos. 6114–6117) published by Cardinal Angelo Mai, *Spicilegium Romanum,* 1839–1844, vol. IV, pp. 324–339.

John's *Vita* is basically a rendering of the Byzantine *Vita ad Theodorum,* composed by Methodios, who later became Patriarch of Constantinople (d. 846); but John used a separate text of *Stratilates* (see Anrich II, pp. 26–27, 59–61, 84), and youthfully inflated his material with rhetorical wind.

[6] Hunt's article in the *Dictionary of National Biography* is sketchy, and I rely almost exclusively upon William of Malmesbury's *Vita Wulfstani* (ed. Darlington), and upon Florence of Worcester's *Chronicon* for A.D. 1062.

The Nero Manuscript

Critics have found that the appearance of the exotic name Nicholas in the west before the Translation is a more than useful hint of the presence of a cult of St. Nicholas.[7] It is notable that Wulfstan received his pallium through the direct intervention of pope Nicholas II, during the latter's short but effective reign, January 24, 1059–July 27, 1061.[8] Nicholas II and Nicholas I were the two popes before Gregory VII (Hildebrand) who officially chastened the emperor after the model of Nicholas of Myra as depicted in the *Stratilates* legend. There is reason to believe that Nicholas II chose his name upon assuming the papal throne because of this image; nothing is known of the antecedents of Nicholas I.[9]

More indicative of Wulfstan's cult of St. Nicholas is the fact that his favorite pupil, who eventually became prior of Worcester, was named Nicholas (d. 1124).[10] Knowles[11] is one of several who surmise that Nicholas' baptismal name was Aethelred. May we guess that it was Wulfstan who renamed him Nicholas?[12] In his maturity, Wulfstan sent Nicholas to Canterbury to study under Lanfranc.[13] When William of Malmesbury wrote the *Vita Wulfstani*, Nicholas was a primary informant, and Wil-

---

[7] The most scholarly, though not the most comprehensive, study of this aspect is that of Gertrude Franke, *Der Einfluss des Nikolauskultes auf die Namengebung im französischen Sprachgebiet* (Romanische Forschungen, Erlangen, XLVIII.1, 1934): "Kult und Namengebung bilden also sozusagen eine Einheit—das sollen die Ausführungen zeigen" (p. 3).

[8] Darlington, *op. cit.*, pp. xv, xxv.

[9] Of some later relevance is the fact that it was Nicholas II who first authorized the introduction of proses following the gradual of the Mass. Of course the practice had grown up before that date. See Collette, p. 99.

[10] W. Keller, "Die literarischen Bestrebungen von Worcester in A.-S. Zeit," *Quellen und Forschungen* (1900), pp. 88–91, gives a full biography of Nicholas.

[11] Knowles, p. 160, n. 7; Darlington, p. xxxviii, n. 2.

[12] "Clearly, in speaking of the master, our pages should mention his worthy disciple Nicholas, come from one of the best English families. His parents venerated the holy Wulfstan profoundly. They had proof of his friendship in many ways. He baptized their boy; constantly he taught the boy his letters as he grew up, and always had him at his side." (*VW* iii, 17, ed. Darlington, p. 56); cf. p. xxxix. "Nicholas was his particular ward. He afterward became prior of the church of Worcester, following in Wulfstan's steps." (William of Malmesbury, *Gesta Pontificum Anglorum* iv, 147, ed. N.E.S.A. Hamilton, Rolls Series, 1870, p. 287); cf. *VW* iii, 17, p. 57.

[13] The twelfth-century legends of St. Nicholas composed at Bec (*BHL* Nos. 6207–6208) are based on memories of elders who could have been reaching maturity just before Lanfranc departed for England.

liam chided him for not having written the biography himself.[14] In the *Vita* Wulfstan appears to have many of the traits of the legendary St. Nicholas; especially notable is the bald transference from St. Nicholas to Wulfstan of the story of the rescue of sailors.[15] Here then are two important English teachers apparently devoted to St. Nicholas, patron of mariners, travelers, merchants, and bishops, at a moment when, according to recent belief, there was as yet no patronage of scholars. Later I shall indicate where and how this patronage of scholars arose.

William accented Wulfstan's liturgical zeal,[16] and specifically stated: "Cotidie missam cantans, addebat psalterium, omniumque sanctorum memorias, quorum toto anno singula sollennia succedunt singulis, in septem divisas per septem, non omittebat horas." This statement sounds like a direct reference to the Nero manuscript.

Professor Wormald's *English Kalendars Before A.D. 1100*[17] reproduces nineteen Decembers. Except for the possible instance of the Croyland manuscript of "mid s. xi" (Bodleian MS, *Douce 296*), the evidence of those calendars indicates that St. Nicholas Day first appeared in England in the southwest (Sherborne, Wells, and Worcester) in the years before the Conquest, and

---

[14] *VW* iii, 9 and 17. Nicholas' letter to Eadmer, giving details about the mother of Edward the Confessor, is written in the terse and informative prose favored by the best-educated of that generation; see Wm. Stubbs, *Memorials of St. Dunstan*, Rolls Series, 1874, pp. 422–424. William (*VW*, ed. Darlington, p. 57) attributes the important school at Worcester (which produced Coleman, Florence, and John) to Nicholas' discipline; see Knowles, pp. 125, 160. R. W. Southern, *Saint Anselm and His Biographer*, Cambridge, 1963, pp. 314–315, notices Eadmer's "business-like quality" and "freedom from conventional embellishment," as well as his relations with Nicholas (p. 283 n.). This new style, evident in Florence's writing, may have emanated from Nicholas.

[15] *VW* ii, 10 and 19, pp. 42–43, 154–157; cf. p. li. For the English literary tradition of transference of miracles, see my *Saints' Lives and Chronicles*, 1947, p. 61.

[16] *Gesta Pontificum Anglorum* iv, 137–139, ed. Hamilton, pp. 278–289. Dom Anselm Hughes has recently edited a portion of the Cambridge, Corpus Christi College MS *391*, in *The Portiforium of St. Wulstan* (*HBSP*, XC, 1960); the manuscript was transcribed A.D. 1065–1066 (see p. vi). In this second volume (the first is not yet issued) there is no reference to the Nicholas liturgy; but there is (p. 12) a prayer listing 15 patrons of the English, of whom Nicholas is fifteenth. The order suggests that the name of Nicholas may have been added to an original fourteen.

[17] *HBSP*, LXXII, 1934. An English crozier-head with scenes from the Life of St. Nicholas is reproduced in C. J. Godfrey, *The Church in Anglo-Saxon England*, 1962, Pl. 8b: "possibly late Anglo-Saxon."

was a product of Anglo-Saxon, not Norman, activity. The first instances appear in manuscripts copied at cathedrals rather than monasteries, though, to be sure, cathedral rites and customs in England at the time were heavily monastic. In Wormald's *Kalendars After A.D. 1100*[18] every calendar records December 6, St. Nicholas, in red letter or equivalent.

The weight of evidence points directly to Lorraine, not Normandy, as the source of Wulfstan's Nicholas cult. Just before the Conquest, the church in southwestern England was dominated by foreigners, but they were seldom Normans. Leofric of Exeter may possibly have been born in England,[19] but he received his scholastic training in Lorraine. Chancellor for Edward the Confessor, he was rewarded by appointment as bishop of Crediton in 1046. Moving to Exeter in 1050, he expelled the monks and installed canons under the rule of Chrodegang of Metz, "which had been familiar to him in Lotharingia."[20] At least two other southwestern bishops were also from Lorraine. Giso, born in the diocese of Liège, became a clerk of chancery for England by Edward's appointment; the king then created him bishop of Wells in 1060. He was consecrated at Rome by Nicholas II, together with another Lotharingian, Walter, who had been chaplain for Edward's queen Edith. Walter was rewarded with the see of Hereford. When he died in 1079, he was succeeded by Robert Losinga, also of Lorraine.

The relations of Worcester with these adjacent sees were cordial: their bishops had much in common.[21] The four sees are

---

[18] *HBSP*, LXXVII.
[19] F. M. Stenton, *Anglo-Saxon England*, 1947, p. 652.
[20] *Dictionary of National Biography*.
[21] Stenton, *loc. cit.*, and William Stubbs' Introduction to *De Inventione Crucis*, 1861. Relations with Liège were intensified by the alliance of king Edward and emperor Henry III in 1049 against Baldwin of Flanders. Aldred, bishop of Worcester and eventually archbishop of York, who consecrated his successor Wulfstan, was royal legate to Germany, centering at Cologne, in 1054; he received the pallium from Pope Nicholas II at Rome in 1061, together with the Lotharingians Giso of Wells and Walter of Hereford, and almost certainly traveled via Lorraine. Another *de Lotharingia oriundus* was the royal chaplain, Herman, who was rewarded with the see of Ramsbury in 1045 and, after three years' exile at St. Omer, the see of Sherborne in 1058; see Frank Barlow, ed., *The Life of King Edward* (Nelson's Med. Texts, 1962), pp. xlvi ff., 91 ff., and refs.

the first, or among the first, to yield evidence of a cult of St. Nicholas. Three of the four bishops were consecrated by pope Nicholas II or his legates, and three of the four were educated in the imperial schools of Lorraine, which in that generation were the finest in Europe, drawing their strength in large part from the support which the Saxon emperors had given them throughout the late tenth century.

Dewick was the first to substantiate the liturgical flow to England from Lorraine by closely checking and comparing the contemporary Leofric Collectar (British Museum MS *Harl. 2961*) and the Collectar of Wulfstan (Cambridge, *C.C.C.* MS *391*).[22] He found in these two manuscripts "a most remarkable agreement with Liège use... The influence of lower Lorraine is very strongly marked in *Harl. 2961*. There is no trace of the influence of Normandy... We are compelled to think that one of the bishops whom Edward the Confessor brought over from Lorraine must have exercised his *jus liturgicum* in arranging the services of *Harl. 2961*."[23] Of the Collectar of Wulfstan he says: "A compact group of Low Country breviaries therefore shares the tradition with Leofric and Wulfstan. That England has borrowed from abroad there is little doubt."[24] The *sanctorale* in MS *391* has lost the folios from September 29 to December 26, and therefore we cannot know whether it contained the Nicholas liturgy. But of the Liège source for the whole liturgical year in both manuscripts there can be no doubt. Moreover, Dewick[25] has compared the calendar years, not only for these two manuscripts, but also for four other Worcester manuscripts (Oxford, *Hatton 113;* Cambridge, C.C.C. *9;* Oxford, Magdalen, *100;* the Worcester Service Book) written under Wulfstan. Ex-

---

[22] Edited by E. S. Dewick and W. H. Frere, *HBSP,* LVI, 1921. See also Dom G. Morin in *Revue Bénédictine,* XII, pp. 196–198; Dom Fernand Cabrol, *L'Angleterre chrétienne avant les Normands* (1909), pp. 300–301; Antoine Auda, *Étienne de Liège* (Acad. Royale de Belgique, Cl. des Beaux-Arts, Memoires in 8°, II, 1923, i), pp. 39 and 78; H. M. Bannister, *Monumenti Vaticani* II (1913), p. 227.

[23] P. xii.

[24] P. xx.

[25] P. 600.

cept for *391* all have December 6 marked for Nicholas—a full generation before the Day spread through England. Another manuscript of the same period, from Exeter and possibly Leofric's, has a litany containing Nicholas among the confessors.

A final observation. Granted that, in the tradition of Oswald, the cathedrals were claustral, nevertheless, as Darlington points out,[26] the appointments to English sees made by both Edward and the Conqueror were far from overwhelmingly Norman, and neither king favored those of monastic training.[27]

---

[26] R. R. Darlington, "Ecclesiastical Reform in the Late Old English Period," *English Historical Review*, LI (1936), pp. 396, 420.

[27] "When the appointments to the English sees made by William I are examined, it is found that five only of the men promoted were certainly monks, one a secular canon, the origin of another is unknown, and of the remaining eleven, eight were certainly, and three probably promoted for their service in the chancery." Darlington, *VW*, p. 395, n. 3; cf. Knowles, p. 71.

Chapter III

The Text

In the following text I have transcribed *Nero E 1*, normalizing and correcting the orthography and in a few places making verbal substitutions warranted by other manuscripts; but I have not shifted the order of the items, even though I think that the position of several is not that of the originator. In the annotations are only such comparisons with texts which have been published from other manuscripts as will illustrate the varieties of use.[1] Although I have compared the lections with the texts published by Falconius, Lipomanus, and Mai, and with the lections in other manuscripts that have appeared in print, I have not recorded the abundant variants; for nothing short of comparison with a fundamentally new edition of John's *Vita S. Nicolai*—such as will eventually appear in the *Acta SS*—would be informative.[2] Finally I have subjoined some literary texts which document the discussion to follow. I list below those texts which I have compared, together with the letters by which they are identified in the notes.

Compared Texts

A   Georges Durand, ed., *Ordinaire de l'église Notre-Dame Cathédrale d'Amiens par Raoul de Rouvray (A.D. 1291)* (Mem-

---

[1] Most of the shifts no doubt result from differences between secular and monastic offices. Liturgists have not yet satisfactorily dealt with the technicalities involved; but see *Mitrale* IV, 2 and 10 (*Pat. Lat.* CCXIII, 154–155 and 186), composed by Sichard of Cremona, *ca.* 1200, who states the principles. Dom J. Pothier, *Les mélodies grégoriennes d'après la tradition* (1880), pp. 241 ff., clearly defines antiphons and responses as they appear in this discussion. Leroquais' census (*Brév.*) includes about 70 items which present fairly complete texts of the office. Hubert Silvestre, in *Ephemerides Liturgicae,* LXVII (1953), p. 140, n. 1, lists 35 manuscripts of this Nicholas-cursus in various forms, examined by himself or by M. Beyssac, but states that the list represents only a fraction of those available. Some of these have been published, as have some which he did not list.

[2] With the single exception of the lections in H, which are taken from an unknown *vita* which is like Otloh's, each of the texts of the lections (including B.M. MS Arundel 91, *saec.* xii ?, published by Birch, op. cit., pp. 198–201) has been taken directly from the *Vita S. Nicolai* of John of Naples, though the liturgists have sometimes abridged and paraphrased passages for the sake of brevity. No two sets I have examined are identical.

The Text 15

oires de la Société des Antiquaires de Picardie XXII, 1934, pp. 38–41, 284–286). A special Nicholas cult existed at Amiens: Dec. 6, octave, procession; Translation with 9 lections, *inc.: Beatus Nicolaus.* A claustral church was founded 1075 by bp. Drogo. "De nullo confessore agitur inter Pascha et Pentecosten, nisi de sancto Nicolao et de sancto Honorato [patrono], neque de aliqua virgine." Mai 9: "Novem lectiones fiunt de translatione ipsius que sic incipit: *Post obitum beati Nicolai."*

Ab Aberdeen Breviary, II, fos. x^r–xiii^r. A reproduction in facsimile of Chapman and Myllar's edition of 1509–1510. The Scottish Rite as derived from the Sarum use. I have compared with this the *Breviarum Bothanum ... in Scotia* (from a manuscript of *saec.* xv), London, 1900, pp. 450–453. Both contain full lections, the former abbreviating and altering John's text, the latter copying exactly.

1 2 3 4 5 6

B Chevalier, *Bayeux,* pp. 192–194.

Br Facsimile of Bibl. Royale (Brussels) manuscript *Lat. 10066–77* (*saec.* xi² ?, from Liége), fo. 87^r, in Silvestre, p. 146. See *Cat. Cod. Brux.* p. 393.

C Propers of the Mass in London, British Museum manuscript *Cotton Vitellius A XVIII* (Wells, A.D. 1061–1088), fos. 146^v–147^r.

E J. N. Dalton, ed., *Ordinale Exon.* (*saec.* xiv), 4 vols. (*HBSP* XXXVII, XXXVIII, LXIII, LXXIX), 1909–1940.

H J. B. L. Tolhurst, ed., *The Monastic Breviary of Hyde Abbey, Winchester* (from Oxford Bodleian manuscript *Rawlinson e. 1, ca.* 1300), vol. IV, Sanctorale (*HBSP* LXXVIII), 1939, fos. 397–400. A complete *historia,* with unique lections.

L Chevalier, *Laon,* pp. 206 ff. (*saec.* xii/xiii). "Ab antiquo." The incipit for lections is, "Nicholaus ex illustri prosapia ortus"— *BHL,* No. 6150 (John) or *BHL* 6126 (Otloh's M). There was a Nicholas chapel at Laon cathedral, to which a procession moved after 1 Vespers.

N *Nero E 1.*

S *Antiphonale Sarisburiense* (Plainsong and Medieval Music Society, Fasc. xiii, xiv, 1908), Facsimile Plates 354–362 (*saec.* xiii). Fairly represents "Sarum Use"; cf. Ab, B, E; 3 anthems and 3 responses for each Nocturn, 6 anthems for Lauds.

V   Dom Louis Brou, ed., *The Monastic Ordinale of St. Vedast's Abbey, Arras,* II (*HBSP* LXXXVII, 1955), p. 215. The Nocturns not given: "Invitatorum, hymnum, antiphone, versus et responsoria, sicut in libris. Evangelium cum omelia *Homo quidam nobilis.*"

W   *Paléographie Musicale* XII (1922), Plates 238–242. Facsimiles of Worcester manuscript *F 160* (*saec. xiii*). Follows the order of Y exactly except that one response (11) and the Proses are omitted, and the order of two anthems is reversed; consequently I have not recorded variants from this text.

Y   Karl Young, *Manly* pp. 259–263, from Paris, Bibl. Nat. manuscript *Latin 12584* (*saec.* xi², from St.-Maur-des-Fossés), fos. 383^v–385^v.[3]

ABBREVIATIONS INDICATING LITURGICAL USE

a – anthem
b – lection (*sic:* 8b)
c – anthem added to canticle
d – postcommunion
e – epistle
f – compline
g – gospel
h – prime
i – invitatory
j – terce
l – lauds

m – mass
n – nocturns (*sic:* 1n = 1st noct.)
o – prayer, collect
p – procession
r – response
s – secret
t – rubric
v – vespers
x – Translation (May 9)
z – nones

I have noted (in Pitra's modern Latin translation) analogous passages from three Byzantine hymns to Nicholas, edited by Cardinal J. B. Pitra, *Analecta Sacra* (Spicilegium Solesmense), *Parata I* (Paris, 1876): one of *saec.* viii/ix attributed to the sixth-century hymnographer Romanos, pp. 202–209; the second, pp. 355–358, generally attributed to Theodore the Studite (759–826), though rejected by Anrich, II, pp. 360–362, who would place it in *saec.* ix²; the third, of uncertain date and authorship, pp. 613–614. The composer of the liturgy seems not to have used

---

[3] L. Delisle in *Bibliothèque de l'École des Chartes,* XXVIII (1867), p. 371, says that *12584* was already in St. Germain-des-Prés in *saec.* xi/xii. Another antiphonary, *Lat. 12601,* which Delisle calls *saec.* xii, but Auda (p. 47) *saec.* xi¹, has the same origin and history; it contains proper offices for many saints of western cult, including (p. 178) Nicholas. I have not examined it, nor do I know why Young failed to use it.

The Text

these particular hymns. However, their verbal effect may exist to some degree in the liturgy, and No. 56 and No. 57, which do not depend upon John, may echo some lost Greek hymns of similar tradition.[4] Since I can adduce no evidence from the exact phrasing, I have chosen to use the modern Latin translation.

I
OCTAVA IDUS DECEMBER NATALE SANCTI NICHOLAI PONTIFICIS

2

Ad Vesperas. [A] O pastor eterne, O clemens et bone custos qui dum devoti gregis preces adtenderes voce lapsa de celo presuli sanctissimo dignum episcopatu Nicholaum ostendisti tuum famulum.

v,a.   v,c—Ab.   x,a—A.   v,a in Ab,L is *Iustum deduxit*.

Ps.-Romanos, Str. 1 (p. 202): Apud Myros, O sancte, sacrorum factus es antistes; hodie enim, postquam Christi, implevisti evangelium, posuisti tuam animam pro populo tuo; insontes fecisti salvos ab interitu; idcirco sanctus effectus es, O magne minister divinae gratiae. *5 (p. 203)*: Pastor ille bonus agnos convocavit suamque fecit praedam, eos in ovile voce duxit, ereptos ex faucibus alienigenae quem communem omnibus hostem valida funda confodit ... *25 (p. 209)*: ... tantum enim vales ab Eo qui solos omnia fecit, in Deo qui etiam nunc virtutem suis largitur servis, sicuti magna voce propheta canit ...

Johannes Diaconus (Mombr. 299.35): Sic conversi ad Deum flagitabant ex intimis praecordiis, ut pastor aetaernus utillissimum suarum ovium pastorem ostendere dignaretur. Illis quippe summa cum devotione orantibus vocem de caelo audivit dicentem sibi praedictus pontifex.

Namur MS, 15 (Anal. Boll. II, p. 144, lines 36–9): Sed *pastor aetern*us, *clemens et bon*us *custos, cum devoti gregis preces attend*isset, *voce lapsa de caelo ostend*it *praesuli sanctissimo* illum *episopatu dignum* esse qui primus nocturno tempore ad ecclesiam occurreret, atque subjungit quod Nicolaus nomen ejus foret.

---
[4] Wilhelm Meyer, "Anfang und Ursprung der lateinischen und griechischen rhythmischen Dichtung," *Gesammelte Abhandlungen zur mittellateinischen Rhythmik*, II (Berlin, 1905), pp. 1–201, esp. pp. 87–88.

3

INVITATORIUM. Adoremus Regem seculorum in quo vivit Nicholaus honor sacerdotum.

i. (vitatoria—N) Followed by psalm *Venite* and hymn in some manuscripts.

Ps.-Romanos, 10 (p. 205): Tu, bone Deus, qui tellurem super aquas fundasti, firma mentem meam in timore tuo, Domine, ut dicam et agam quae mihi prosint, et enuntiem vitam praestantem praesulis Myrorum ... *2 (p. 202)*: Christo offert hostiam immaculatam, integerrimam, Deo acceptam; pontifex siquidem impollutus tam mente quam carne; unde adest merito Ecclesiae patronus eiusque vindex, magnus minister divinae gratiae. *3 (p. 203)*: En igitur nunc in hac die pontifici sacra, O populi, splendida illustremur panegyri, et modulemur hymnam Christo Salvatori. Christus enim eum gloria adornavit, mortalibusque dedit magnum sidus omnibus luculentum ...

4
SUPER NOCTURNO

[A] Nobilissimis siquidem natalibus ortus velut lucifer Nicholaus emicuit.

in, 1a. 2v, a—H,V.

Ps.-Romanos, 3 (p. 203): ... mortalibusque dedit magnum sidus omnibus luculentum, sacrum scilicet mysteriorum suorum opificem ... *6 (p. 204)*: Amictu virtutis palam circumductus, ut alter Moyses, tu gratia multus, O Nicolae pater, densam in nubem ivisti, sublimi gressu per incessa loca transibas, O longe decore, Dei gloria irradiatus ...

S. Theodoros Studites, 3 (p. 356): Totus orbis, ac si novum sidus effulget, in hac tua memoria, O sapiens, lumine perfusus festum agit, gaudet, gloriatur, mente suspiciens sacra prodigia.

Auctor Anon., 4 (p. 614): Salve, sidus, illuminans jacentes in nocte.

Johannes Diaconus (Mombr. 297.16-18): ... parentes eius inter catervas potentum quanto maiore honorificentia celebrabantur. tanto supernae patriae accensi desyderio. magis caelestis quam terrenae dignitatis gloriam appetebant.

Ghent MS 305, p. 261 (Boll. Subsidia Hagiog., 25, 1948, p. 70): ... beatus Nicholaus inter spiritales patres velut lucifer inter astra fulgida coeli luminis singularis effulsit.

5

A. Postquam domi puerilem decursat etatem, cunctis mundi huius spretis delectationibus, Christi se iugo subiciens documentis sanctis suum prebuit auditum.

1n, 2a. 1n, 4a—H,Y. v, a(7 Dec.)—A.

Ps.-Romanos, 11 (p. 205): Decreto fatidico natus es, sacratissime, statimque pedibus stetisti rectus, O Nicolae, eo ipso significans te conculcaturum esse superbientem draconis ferociam, eiusque immensam nequitiam esse cohibiturum, ne etiam nunc erumpat in eos qui ad te fidenter confugiunt ...

Johannes Diaconus (Mombr. 297.41–45): Puerilibus igitur annis ut patriarcha Iacob simpliciter domi transactis coepit bonae indolis adolescens esse, et non sicut illa nunc solus ecclesiarum tenebat limina. Et quod ibi patulo de scripturis advertebat auditu, non immemor armariolo pectoris recondebat.

6

A. Pudore repletus bono [dono—N] Dei famulus sumptibus datis stupri nefas prohibuit.

1n, 3a. 1n, 1a—S. 1n, 6a—H,Y. v, a(Dec. 7, 8)—A. z, a—L.

Ps.-Romanos, 20 (p. 207): Sordes vitae effugiens, innocentiam induisti ... in quo impolluti, O pater, mactasti agnum Dei, universae terrae visus es alter Aaron, stolam non lavans, at expugnans calamitates fidelissimae tuae gentis ...

Johannes Diaconus (Mombr. 297.47–51): ... et cum anhelaret ad perficiendum: quod pio vertebat in pectore: iuvenilis formido coepit titillare mentem: ne borealis aura perceleret. quidquid pro Christo facere disponebat Haec secum ad deum verum totum desiderii sui pandens velamen deprocabatur: ut ille qui habet omnium scientiam: inspiraret ... *(297.58–298.1):* ... condoluit miserrimo homo: atque virginum execrans stuprum ...

7

A. Auro virginum incestus auro patris [patri—N] earum inopiam auro prorsus utrorumque detestabilem infamiam Dei servus ademit Nicholaus.

1n, 4a. 2n, 1a—Ab,B,E,H,S,Y. l, a(Dec. 8)—A.

Johannes Diaconus (Mombr. 298.1–8): Decrevit omnino ex suis abundantiis earum supplere inopiam, ne puellae nobilibus ortae natalibus lupanari macularentur infamia ... Eia famule dei exime pauperiem patris exime filiarum scortum tellus tuae mentis hactenus sancto exculta vomere, duplum subito prorumpat in fructum, ut ex uno famelici satietur ingluvies, et ex alio virginum redimatur incoestus.

Wolferius, Vita Godehardi (Mon. Germ. Hist., *Script. IV, pp. 207–208*): [Godehardus] providerit more quidem et exemplo sancti sui patrono Nycolai episcopi, qui elemosinarum *auro* et *virginum incestus* et *patris earum inopiam* et totius familiae *detestabilem ademit infamiam.*

Ghent MS 289 *(Liber beate Marie de Camberone, saec. xii; Cat. Cod. Hagiog. Gandav., Subsidia Hagiog., 25, p. 157)*: ...qui auro virginum pudorem *(cf. No. 6 above)* redemit earumque patris inopiam fugavit...

8

A. Innocenter puerilia iura transcendens, evangelice institutionis discipulus [-lis—N] effectus est.

1n, 5a.   2n, 2a—Ab,B,E,H,S,Y.   v, a(Dec. 8)—A.

Johannes Diaconus (Mombr. 297.45–47): Ubi autem utroque parente orbatus est, saepius illud evangelicum ante suae mentis oculos ducebat: Nisi quis renunciaverit omnibus quae possidet, non potest meus esse discipulus. *(297.41–45)*: Puerilibus igitur annis ut patriarcha Iacob simpliciter domi transactis coepit bonae indolis adolescens esse: et non sicut illa aetas assolet lascivias complexus est mundi: sed nunc parentum comitatus vestigiis: nunc solus ecclesiarum terebat limina: Et quod ibi patulo de scripturis advertebat auditu,... armariolo pictoris recondebat. *(Mombr. 298.50–52)*: O virum omni imbutum peritia omnique instructum scientia: qui ut se utrumque testamentum suscipere profiteretur: non est contentus lege litterae: sed annectit evangelicam gratiam...

9

A. Gloriam mundi sprevit cum suis oblectationibus et ideo meruit provehi ad summum sacerdotii gradum.

1n, 6a.   2n, 3a—Ab,E,H,S,Y.

Ps.-Romanos, 1 (p. 202): Apud Myros, O sancte, sacrorum factus es antistes; hodie enim, postquam Christi, implevisti evangelium, posuisti tuam animam pro populo tuo; insontes fecisti salvos ab interitu; idcirco sanctus effectus es, O magne minister divinae gratiae.

Johannes Diaconus (Mombr. 299.24): Noluit quoque seculi captare famam, ne sanctorum contubernio privaretur. *(300.1–3)* ... vox de caelo iussit ut coram templi foribus excubaret, quatenus ibidem dignum deo et ecclesiae suae sanctae quod utile feret reperiret episcopum.

10

I [LECTIO]
QUALITER EGREGIUS DOMINI PRESUL
NICHOLAUS · CULMEN AD HONORIS
EST RAPTUS PONTIFICALIS

Myrrhea metropolis orbata est suo antistite; eius obitum non mediocriter adiacentium parrochiarum condolentes episcopi, fuerat enim bene religiosus. Convenerunt in unum cum clericis cunctis, ut alium annuente Domino providerent illi [ille—N] aecclesiae secundum scita canonum presulem idoneum. Concione itaque facta intererat quidam pontifex magnae auctoritatis, ad cuius intuitum omnium pendebat sententia, ut quem ille voce proderet, hunc procul dubio elegerent universi. Hic ergo per omnia sequens apostolorum vestigia cunctos ieiuniis et devotissimis precibus hortatus est insistere quatinus ille qui Mathiam indidit numerum supplere apostolicum ipse solita clementia pandere dignaretur quem vellet fungi tanto sacerdotio.

Johannis Neapolitensis Vita Nicolai (Mombritius 299.26–35.)

11

RESPONSORIA II

Confessor Dei Nicholaus nobilis pro genere sed nobilior moribus, ab ipso puerili [-libus N] evo secutus Dominum meruit divina revelatione ad summum provehi sacerdotium. V. Erat enim valde compatiens et superafflictos pia gestans viscera. Meruit.

1n, 1r. 3n, r—B. x—A.

Cf. 4, 5, 8, 9, and below p. 59

Thiofrid of Echternach (d. A.D. 1110; cf. Manitius III, 95–96), in his *Flores Epitaphii Sanctorum* iii, 5 (*Pat. Lat.* CLVII, 380C), which he dedicated to apb. Bruno of Trier, used the Nicholas myrrh as the central illustration of his theme of "odor of sanctity," and quoted the *praeconium:* "Erat enim valde compatiens, et pia super afflictos gestans viscera pietatis et misericordiae", with special reference to the legend noted below, pp. 45-46.

12

[II LECTIO] Tunc omnes quasi caelesti commonerentur [-niti—N] oraculo, sic conversi ad Deum flagitabant ex intimis precordiis, ut pastor aeternus utillimum ovium suarum pastorem ostendere dignaretur. Illis quippe summa cum devotione orantibus, vocem de caelo audivit predictus pontifex dicentem sibi ut egrediens ante portas aecclesiae staret, et quem primum hora matutinali venire conspiceret, ipsum consecrarent antistitem, adiungens etiam quod Nicholaus vocaretur. Tunc presul ille ceteris coepiscopis hanc insinuans revelationem. "Credo enim quod non privemur promisso Dei," sic ait; et valvas basilicae [ianuas asyli—Mombr., Lipomanus] sancta calliditate observabat. Mirum in modum! matutinali hora quasi a Deo missus ante omnes se agebat Nicholaus.

(*Mombritius 299.35-44.*)

13

R. Operibus sanctis Nicholaus [-lao—N] humiliter insistens [-tent—N] revelatione divina provectus est ad summam sacerdotii gradum. V. Voce quippe de celo lapsa cuidam insinuatur presuli dignum episcopatu Nicholaum. Ad sum.

1n, 2r. in, 1r—H. 1n, 4r—Y. v, *capit.*—L.

Johannes (Mombr. 299.43-44): Mirum in modum matutinali hora quasi a domino missus se ante omnes agebat Nicolaus. *(299.37-40):* ...vocem de caelo audivit dicentem sibi praedictus pontifex...ipsum consecrarent antistitem, adiungens etiam quod Nicolaus vocitaretur.
  ...ad summam sacerdotii gradum (see 11, above).

14

[III LECTIO] Cumque ad ecclesiae ianuas propinquasset, iniecta manu eum apprehendit episcopus, blanditerque sciscitatus

The Text 23

est, dicens, "Quale nomen habes?" Ille columbina ut erat simplicitate, inclinato capite, "Nicholaus," inquit, "servus vestrae sanctitatis." Cui protinus presul, palmis innexis, ait, "Fili, veni mecum, est enim aliquod secreti quod tue indoli fari debeam." Mox introgressus, en fratres proclamavit: "Vere, ait Dominus, quodcumque petieritis in nomine meo, credite quia accipietis, et fiet vobis. En, inquam, quod petivimus acceptimus. En adest de quo vestra flagitavit caritas." Quo viso ingentem omnes tulere clamorem ad sidera, et certatim Salvatoris laudabant magnalia. Episcopi laetabant pro collegii celitus collato; clerici alludebant sicut bone pecudes. Quod multis moror? Licet plurimum obstitent et renitens plurimumque repugnaverit. Inthronizatus ilico sicut mos exigebat, regionis illius pontificalem accepit infulam.

(Mombritius 299.44-55.)

15

R. Quadam die tempestate saevissima quassati nautae coeperunt sanctum vocare Nicholaum. Et statim [testatim—N] cessavit tempestas. V. Mox illis clamantibus apparuit quidam dicens illis, "Ecce adsum; quid vocastis me?" Et statim.

1n, 3r. 2n, 1r—Y. 2n, 2r—H.

Johannes (Mombr. 300.28-30): Quadam vero die cum quidam nautae subita maris tempestate periclitarentur ... clamitabant: "Nicolae famule Dei ..." *(300.33-34)*: Mira res. Talia referentibus apparuit quidam in similitudine viri dicens eis: "Vocastis enim me, ecce assum."

Namur MS 15 (Anal. Boll. II, pp. 145.4-8): Nam quidam *nautae* qui nomen tantum viri Dei et gratiam curationum ejus audierant, cum fuissent *quassati saevissima tempestate, coeperunt sanctum Nicolaum* invocare. Et *clamantibus illis, apparuit quidam* sub ipsius sancti viri schemate, *dicens eis: Vocastis me, ecce adsum.* Mox adiuvit eos celere sublevatione, et *cessare* fecit *tempesta*tem superveniente inaestimabile tranquillitate.

16

[IIII LECTIO] Mira prorsus, mira et stupenda sunt que narrantur, et si fas est antiquis per omnia comparanda. Quondam enim Samuheli prophete sanctus precepit spiritus ut ad domum Isai pergeret, unumque ex eius filiis placitum Domino regem inungeret. Modo autem isti ex intimo precanti affectu. Vox de caelo iussit ut coram templi foribus excubaret, quatinus ibidem dignum Deo et ecclesiae sanctae profici eum repperint antistitem. Illi quamquam videnti locus tantum non regis nomen predicitur, huic et locus et nomen presulis declaratur. Ille caput regium cornu roboravit [iṇroraū—N] olei; iste super caput Nicholai virtutem invocavit spiritus sancti. Sed tamen et rex et presul uterque est electus a Domino. Unde nos minime irridendi sumus, qui magnis ausi fuimus componere parua. Hinc iam ad ea quae in episcopatu gessit, opitulante Domino vertatur stilus.

(*Mombritius 299.56–300.8*)

17

R. Audiens Christi confessor trium iuvenum innocentum necem precurrit quantotius ad locum quo fuerant [-at—N] plectendi et liberavit eos. V. Statimque solutos a vinculis usque ad pretorium iudicis secum adduxit. Et libera.

1n, 4r.   2n, 1r—Ab,B,E,S.   2n, 2r—Y.   2n, 3r—H.

S. Theodoros Studites, 6 (p. 356): Quis alius similis visus est adesse oppressis et jactatis inter discrimina, sicut tu olim, O beati Dei? Canunt enim te abacti juvenes in necem injustam, tres oves tuae...

Johannes Diaconus (Mombr. 302.37–41): Ecce relatum est a dicentibus: "Domine sancte si tua praesto fuisset in civitate paternitas: nullo modo iniuste fieret trium militum caedes. Nam et cives omnes valde vestram condoluerunt absentiam, quoniam consul magno excaecatus munere, neci eorum consensit. Quibus auditis vir domini pietatis igne inflamatus; praefatos rogavit principes, ut cum illo rapidis festinarent passibus. (*Mombr. 302.53–58*): Eminusque de manu eius gladium propellens, nec prius abscessit quam illos solutos a vinculis secum reduceret, repetens, me me, inquam, nam pro istis innocenter condemnatis paratus sum dedere leto... Ad praetorium proconsulis accessit. (*Mombr. 304.20*): Recordatus est qualiter sanctus Nicolaus iuvenum liberator trium mirabilis fuisset...(.23–24): Quatenus sicut eius instantia tres illos erutos a morte conspeximus, ita nos per eius intercessionem ab instanti eripiamur sententia.

The Text

Namur MS 15 (p. 145.34-42): **Audiens** etiam *Christi confessor trium* puerorum *innocentum necem, praecucurrit quantocius ad locum quo fuerant plectandi,* astante magna multitudine propter exitus expectationem... sed *statim solutos a vinculis usque ad praetorium* consulis *secum adduxit* ... ab imminenti periculo *eos liberavit.*

18
IN SECUNDO NOCTURNO

A. Pontifices almi divina revelatione laetificati [glorificati—N] Nicholaum tunc presulem devotissime consecraverunt [-ti erunt N].

1n, 1a.   2n, 4a—Y.   3n, 1a—Ab,B,E,S.   3n, 4a—H.

Johannes Diaconus (Mombr. 299.55): Episcopi laetabantur... super thronum impositus est illico, et sicut mox [mos] est illius regionis pontificalem accepit insulam [infulam]. *(299.37-40)*: Illis summa cum devotione orantibus vocem de caelo audivit dicentem sibi praedictus pontifex ut... ipsum consecrarent antistitem, adiungens etiam quod Nicolaus vocitaretur.

Namur MS 15 (p. 144.39-41): ... subjungit quod *Nicola*us nomen ejus foret. Hunc quaesitum et inventum, *devotissime tunc praesulem consecraverunt pontifices almi, divina revelatione laetificati.*

19

A. Sanctus quidem triticum quod a nautis postulaverat acceptum et sagacitate distribuit [-ebat—N] et [ex—N] augeri precibus impetravit.

2n, 2a.   2n, 5a—Y.   3n, 2a—Ab,B,E,S.   3n, 5a—H.

Ps.-Romanos, 17 (p. 207): Iosephem sapientem imitatus, O praeclare, ut ille, sic tu nutrivisti populos et satiasti. Immo plus quam olim nunc factum est: ille enim frumentum distribuit ubertim indigentibus.

Johannes Diaconus (Mombr. 300.56-57): ... adveniens Nicolaus, nautis infit, "Vos rogaturus accessi ut populo huic tabe diuturnae famis laboranti consulentes." *(301.1-2)*: "et modo hoc triticum deferimus per ministrorum manus in augustalium stipendii metiendum." *(301.12-16)*: Vir itaque Dei accepto frumento, sic per industriam illud partiri studuit, sicut unumquemque noverat indigere. Mirandis plus miranda succedunt. Tanta enim omnipotens

Dei largitate hoc ipsum parum quod sanctus distribuit auctum est, ut non tantum eodem sed etiam altero exacto anno ad victum singulis sufficeret.

20

[A.] Muneribus datis neci sunt iuvenes innocentes [-ter—N] addicti quibus Domini servus fuit vite presidium festinanter.

2n, 3a. 2n, 6a—Y. 3n, 3a—Ab,B,E,S. 3n, 6a—H. v, a(Dec. 11)—A.

S. Theodoros Studites, 6 (p. 356): Canunt enim te abacti juvenes in necem iniustam, tres oves tuae.

Johannes Diaconus (Mombr. 302.37-41): "Domine sancte... nullo modo iniuste fieret trium militum caedes... quoniam consul magno excaecatus munere, neci eorum consensit." Quibus auditis vir domini pietatis igne inflamatus, praefatos rogavit principes ut cum illo rapidis festinarent passibus.

Ps.-Johannes Diaconus (Mombr. 309.6-7): "... sicut liberavit tres illos innocentes de laqueo mortis et de ira Constantini imperatoris, et ad salutem adduxit, ita filium nostrum revocabit." (*Legenda Gethronis*)

21

A. Iam decus lactentium [laet- —N] Nicholaus mirabili portendebat auspitio sancte parsimonie tempus.

2n, 4a. 1n, 3a—H,Y.

Johannes Diaconus (Mombr. 297.25-27): In ipso ita dicam primordio nativitatis eius monstrare dignatus est, enim vero cum matris adhuc lacte aleretur, coepit bino in hebdomade die quarta scilicet et sexta feria semel bibere mammas. (*297.38-39*): Quis enim audit parvulum in die semel et non amplius papilas bibere matris, et facile credit? (*300.12-13*): corpus ieiuniis macerabat.

22

A. Qui[hic—all other MSS]dum matris adhuc lacte nutriretur, quarta et sexta feria semel in die papillas bibebat.

2n, 5a. 1n, 2a—H.

See 21 and 34.

23

[A.] Ad quantam vero messem divina convaluerem in eo semina sequentia pietatis opera profitentur.

2n, 6a. 1n, 5a—H,Y.

The Text

Johannes Diaconus (Mombr. 305.57–58): ... tanta quottidie miracula exhibet ut nulla carnis sufficiat lingua referre.

24

[V LECTIO] Pontificali igitur cathedra sublimatus eandem morum gravitatem quam prius, eandemque sequebatur humilitatem. Creber in oratione pervigilabat, corpus attenuabat ieiuniis, mulierum consortia licet ab ipso pueritie suae tempore exhorruerit, tamen quandam ex hoc quasi pestem fugiebat. In suscipiendis hominibus humilem, in loquendo se prebebat efficacem. Alacer erat in exhortando, severus in corripiendo. Viduarum et orphanorum atque oppressorum sic negotia curabat ac si propria essent. Rapinam execrabatur potentium; arguebat violentos [vinolentos—N]; et si quem forte quolibet casu affectum cernebat, mirabiliter reficiebat mirabiliusque consolabatur.

(Mombritius 300.11–19.) Cf. Mon. Germ. Hist., *Scriptorum T. XXXII,* p. 132.

25

R. Beatus Nicholaus iam triumpho potitus novit [non te—N] suis famulis praebere caelestia commoda qui toto corde poscunt eius petitiones, illi nimirum tota nos devotione oportet committere. V. Ut apud Christum eius patrociniis adiuvemur semper. Illi nimirum.

2n, 1r. 2n, 3r—B (no Prose); Ab,E,S (with Prose). 3n, 2r—H. v, p—A. x, r—A.
   Prose: Oportet devota sinceriter
      Peccatores Christianos tenaciter
      Presuli tanto committere. (Chevalier, *Repert.* IV, 262, No. 39775.)

Ps.-Romanos, 21 (p. 208): ... conspicuum te dares, utque post obitum, ut vivens, accurreres et a periculis eos redimeres qui cum fide nomen tuum in discriminibus, O Nicolae...

Johannes Diaconus (Mombr. 306.13–15): Qualis sonus? nempe victoriae ac triumphi, quia dum suis supplicibus collata caellitus non denegant patrocinia, ostendunt se mundi devicto principe, diademate redimitos aeterno. *(306.17–25):* Quoniam si nos ille concorditer festinos inspexerit, favet, credite mihi favet, nostrae devotione... Omnis ergo sexus, omnisque conditio, protectionis eius tutamen expectet, imploret sufragia, quaerat auxilia. Novit enim olim caelesti palma potius misericorditer subvenire afflictis liberare oppressos et pestiferos soluere nexus. His ita praemissis effundamus aliquantulum coram illo precem, ut in fine pagellae patrociniis eius fruamur. Oramus itaque te sanctissime pater Nicolae, ut humillimas nostrae petitionis voces attendas...

26

[VI LECTIO] Crescebat cotidie fama bonitatis eius que ubique laudem ferebat Nicholai. Hinc potens, hinc impotens illum nominabat. Gaudebat populus cunctus [-tis—N] de tali patrono; letabantur heroes de tanto pontifice, qui ita [quinta—N] se auctoritate et gratia plenum exhibebat ut et omnium curam gereret, et episcopi dignitatem non amitteret. Verum tempus me deficiet, quin et sermo deserit si de singulis eius meritis scribere temptavero. Sed qui scire volverit [voluent—N] qualem se quantumque prestiterit, mordacem comprimat dentem et ex subiectis evidenter agnoscere valebit. Cum igitur omnium karismatum virtute corroboraretur [-borantur—N] Nicholaus, et nichil sibi sed totum Dei gratiae tribueret, coepit ita coruscare miraculis ut non tantum sui sed etiam alieni quibuslibet oppressi angustiis, invocato nomine eius statim sentirent levamen.

(Mombritius 300.19-28.)

27

R. Quantam denique messem in eo divina semina creaverunt innumera pietatis officia quibus cotidie strenuus insudabat praeconantur. V. Transitoriam felicitatem quanti pendent et celestis regni gloriam. Innumera.

2n, 2r. 1n, 3r—H,Y. v, a—A.

Cf. 23.

Johannes Diaconus (Mombr. 297.17-18): Tanto supernae patriae accensi desyderio, magis caelestis quam terrenae dignitatis gloriam appetebant.

28

VII [LECTIO] Quadam vero die cum quidam nautae subita maris tempestate periclitarentur, adeo ut presentem illis intemptarent omnia mortem, extemplo dissolutis frigore membris clamitabant: "Nicholae famule Dei, si vera sunt quae de te audivimus, nunc nos ea suppremo in periculo constituti experiamus, quatinus erepti ex sevientis fluctibus maris, Deo et tue liberationi gratias agamus." Mira res! Talia referentibus, apparuit quidam in similitudinem viri, dicens eis, "Vocastis me: ecce adsum." Et coepit eos in rudentibus et antennis aliisque adiuvare navis armamentis. Nec multo post omnis *pelagi cecidit fragor* omnisque cessavit tempestas. Tum laeti nautae pacata sulcantes aequora, quantotius optatum subeunt portum. Qui egressi, sciscitabantur ubi Nicholaus esset. Cum autem indicatus fuisset eis in aecclesia, e vestigio ingressi—mirabile dictu!—quem numquam noverant sine indice cognoverunt.

(*Mombritius 300.28–39*); cf. *Aeneid* i, 154. B (*p. 293*): Sex prime lectiones et due ultime de vita ejus, vii^a de omelia evangelii *Homo quidam peregre,* quam fecit beatus Gregorius papa. [Gregorii Magni, Homilia in Evangelia I, ix, Dies sancti Silvestri (*Pat. Lat.* LXXVI, 1105–09). Matt. xxv, 14–30.]

29

R. Qui cum audissent sancti Nicholai nomen statim expandunt manus utrasque [*om.*—N] ad celum, Salvatoris laudantes clementiam. V. Clara quippe voce coram omnibus dignum referebant illum Dei famulum. Salvat.

2n, 3r. 2n, 2r—Ab,B,E,S. 2n, 4r—H. 2v, r—H.

Johannes Diaconus (Mombr. 305.12–18): Tunc Augustus, "Nostis," inquit, "aliquem hominem cui Nicolas nomen est?" Mox illi, audito tanto nomine, tendentes ad sydera palmas utrasque voce magna dicebant, "Benedictus es, Domine Deus Nicolai sancti, qui non relinquis sperantes in te, et de tua misericordia praesumentes; benedictus es et laudabilis in secula, qui clementer infelices tuos servos dignatus es respicere. Et nunc, Domine, Domine, miserere nostri, et famuli tui Nicolai intercessione eripe nos ab hac perditione."

Namur MS 15 (II, 146.35): Qui cum exposuissit visionem ... mox illi, ut *audi*erunt *nomen sancti Nicolai, expandunt manus utrasque ad coelum, Salvatoris laudantes clementiam,* qui defendit semper ad se clamantium innocentiam, et facit electorum suorum vindictam. Et *clara voce coram omnibus dignum referebant illum Dei famulum.*

30

VIII [LECTIO] Mox prostrati ad pedes eius, coeperunt ei gratias agere dicentes qualiter de confinio mortis episcopo [ipso—N]suffragante liberati essent. Quibus sanctus: "Non meae," inquit, "possebilitatis arbitremini esse quod factum est. Solita Dei est misericordia qua [qui—N] propter credulitatem vestrae fidei vobis succurrere dignatus est clementia. Discite ergo quanti valeat apud Deum fides pura, et petitio non ficta. Propter peccata enim nostra cotidie flagellamur. Tamen si ex toto corde ad bonum Dominum conversi fuerimus, viscera misericordiae suae ilico super nos commovet, et eripit de inminentibus penis vel periculis. Idcirco, fratres, non pigeat nos benefacere sectari humilitatem et [om.—N] libenter pauperibus succerrere. Credite meae parvitati quia ex quo homo in huius mundi voraginem propter delicta sua deiectus est, nullum eius bonum sic Deus approbare legitur, sicut elimosinam si tamen non ob mundi fiat gloriam." His aliisque talibus instructi, admirantes humilitatem spiritus habitus vilitatem [inlit- —N] sermonis facundiam atque magnitudinem virtutis eius discesserunt.

(Mombritius 300.39–51.)

31

R. Ex eius tumba marmore sacrum resudat oleum quo liniti [limiti—N] sanantur ceci surdis auditus redditur et debilis quisque sospes regreditur [resiliet—N]. V. Catervatim ruunt populi cernere cupientes que per eum fiunt mirabilia et debilia [-lis—N]. [Surdis.]

2n, 4r. See Chevalier, *Repert.* IV, 127, No. 37128. With Prose, *Sospitati* (post *Gloria patri* percantato responsono loco *Te Deum* a toto choro alternatim)—Ab,E. 3n, 2r—Ab. 3n, 3r (with *Sospitati*)—B,L,S. 3n, 4r—H; with Prose *Sospes*—Y (in margin, later hand, *Sospitati*). 1v, p—A,Ab,B,L (with *Sospitati*). 2v, r—B,Y. x, r and p—A. The *miraculum Brientii,* whose paralyzed limbs were healed at Saint-Nicolas, Angers (*Cat. Cod. Paris.* III, 158–162), indicates that *Ex eius tumba* came after *lectio xii.*

The Proses

    Sospes nunc efficitur, Nicolae famulans Domino,
    Et qui tuo devote desiderat obtentu salvari.

The Text

       Sospitati dedit aegros olei perfusio
       Nicolaus naufragantum affuit presidio.
       Relevavit a defunctis defunctum in bivio.
       Baptizatur auri viso Iudeus indicio.
       Vas in mare mersum patri redditur cum filio.
       O quam sanctum Dei probat farris augmentatio.
       Ergo laudes Nicolao concinnat haec concio,
       Nam qui corde poscit illum propulsato vitio.

(S reverses lines 4–5; Ab reverses lines 5–6)

The Processions

B (p. 193): Post vesperas fit processio ad altere beati Nicholai ordinata, sicut in dominica, cum fit de matutina, sed sine dracone, sacerdote etiam in suppellicio tantum et capa serica incedente. Eundo cantatur R. *Ex eius tumba* cum suo versu; deinde inchoata ant. *O Xpisti* ab archichoro ex precepto cantoris, sequitur ps. *Magnificat* et oratio *Deus qui beatum.* [Sequentibus *Dominus vobiscum* et *Benedicamus,* et similiter in aliis processionibus consimilibus.—ed. note] Redeundo cantatur aliqua antiphona de beata Virgine, quam non sequitur oratio.

E (I, 201): Ad Vesperas ... Or. *Deus qui beatum Nicholaum.* Memoria de sancto Andrea, de Adventu, et de sancta Maria. Tunc eat processio ad altare sancti Nicholai, quodam de superiore gradu ex assignacione rectoris principalis incipiente. R. *Ex eius tumba,* et choro responsorium prosequente. V. *Catervatim.* Omnes simul dicant versiculum coram altare sancti Nicholae, require in ANTIPHONARIO CLOPTON [?]. Or. *Deus bonitatis auctor.* In revertendo, de omnibus sanctis.

Ps.-Romanos, 4 (p. 203): Jam tempus est tua referendi facinora: ast nemo par laudibus est enarrandis; Christi quippe vos unguentorum factus es, suavitate omnes perfundens, ad te currentes sub odore gratiae sanctissimi Spiritus, O venerande; mysticum es unguentum, unguentum illuminans eos qui fide ungentur, qui vere divina Christi unctione liniti sunt; hinc viris Myrensibus extitisti patronus, O pontifex summe ...

S. Theodoros Studites, 2 (p. 355): Divino linitum unguento, te Myrorum pontificum, cujus unguenta suaviter perflant mihi ex miraculis, quomodo te canam, peccatis foetans, O sancte Nicolae?

Johannes Diaconus (Mombr. 305.58–306.3): Quis enim digne potest explicare qualiter eius meritis promerentibus cecis visus, surdis auditus, et, ut breviter dicam, debilibus cunctis et celerrima et optima redditur valitudo. Quis, inquam, tante est facundiae ut facile possit exprimere qualiter ex marmore tumuli eius sacrum resudat oleum.

Namur MS 15 (p. 148.30–32): Nam *ex tumba ejus oleum* manat, cujus natura quemadmodum est lucis ministra, sic hujus signi gratia anteactas virtutes illustrat et sequentes comprobat, quia cunctos languidos *sanat.*

32

AD CANTICA. Decantande speciosus Nicholae canticis laudes [*om.*—N] tibi presolvisse fac sit nobis utile.

3n, c. iv, a—V. In tercio nocturno. Ant. Decantande...Cantica. Beatus vir. Vs. Iustus et palma.—H.

S. Theodoros Studites, 4 (p. 356): Vere decet: omnium hymnos tuum nomen habet: gratiam enim quum a Deo tuis virtutibus acquisieris, ades omnibus qui cum fide tuam enixe exorant praesentiam; pericula enim solvis, injustos redarguis, ab interitu liberas morte damnatos, judicum iras prodigiose compescens, O beate hierophante, celebrantium te...

33

LECTIO NONA. Quodam autem tempore cum eandem Liciam regionem accolarum pro meritis sic pernitiosa fames oppressit, ut seges aegra victum omnem negaret, mox a provincialibus ruricolis sepedicto famulo Dei pro indigentibus maxime periclitanti, naves triticeis onustae mercibus in litore Arriatici portus adesse nuntiantur. Quo velox adveniens Nicholaus, nautis infit. "Vos rogaturus accessi ut huic populo tabe diuternae famis laboranti consulentes aliquantulum remedii existo frumento inpertiri studeatis." Sic sanctus, et sancto sic aiunt illi, "Non audemus, pater, obsecundare imperatis, quia publica taxatione angariati Alexandriam perreximus; et inde hoc triticum deferimus per ministrorum manus, in augustalia stipendia metiendum." Quibus sanctus, "Audite," inquid, "me, et ne [ine—N] amplius attenuetur hic populus. Per unamquamque ratem saltum centum mihi praebete modios, et ego in Domini mei cui servio virtute spondeo, polliceor, promitto, quia minorationem habebitis apud regium [regnum—N] exactorem. Tandem interventu presulis convicti, ex singulis puppibus centum numeravere modios; et confestim vento surgente secundo classes portum relinquerunt atque spirantibus auris, volucri cursu, Bisantium applicuerunt ad urbem.

(Mombritius 300.52–301.9.)

34

R. Dum vero adhuc penderet ad ubera matris, O nova res, quarta feria et sexta semel in die papillas bibebat. V. Iam quodam modo sacri ieiunii se futurum presignans amatorem Nicholaus. O nova res.

3n, 1r. 2n, 2r—H,Y. 2n, r—A. 1v, r—L,V. x, r—Λ.

Johannes Diaconus (Mombr. 297.26–31): Coepit bino in hebdomade die, quarta scilicet et sexta feria semel bibere mammas... Ecce novi Zacharie vates, ecce alterius Elisabeth filius. *(297.38–39):* Quis enim audit parvulum in die semel et non amplius papillas bibere matris, et facile credit? (Cf. above, 21–22.)

35

LECTIO X. Cum autem integram mensuram quam Alexandriaem susceperant ministris imperatoris numerassent, tantus stupor omnes accepit ut preadmiratione seratim cuncta que facta fuerant, eisdem narrarent ministris. Qua relatione perculsi, Deum rerum omnium auctorem continuata utrique laude magnificabant. Vir itaque Domini accepto frumento sic per industriam illud partiri studuit, sicut unumquemque noverat indigere. Mirandis plus miranda succedunt; tanta enim omnipotentis [-tes—N] Dei largitate, hoc ipsum parum quod sanctus distribuit auctum est ut non tantum eodem sed etiam altero poene exacto anno ad victum singulis sufficeret [-ent—N]. Quin et multi spe credula exinde serere non dubitantes, nequaquam eos expectata seges vanis frustrata est aristis, sed uberibus sparsit [farsit—N] reditibus. Porro nemini hoc incredibile videatur, quia Salvatoris est ista promissio dicentis, "Si habueritis fidem ut granum sinapis, dicetis monti transferre, et transfertur," [Matt. xvii, 19; Luc. xvii, 6] et illud, "Qui in me credit, opera que ego facio et ipse faciet; et maiora horum faciet." [Ioh. xiv, 12] Vere enim in eum credidit Nicholaus, in cuius opitulatione tale tantumque valuit facere miraculum.

(Mombritius 301.9–22.)

36

R. Summe Dei confessor Nicholae te venerantes [tuam catervam te venerantes vides—N] protege namque credimus tuis precibus nos posse [nos. se—N] salvari. V. Qui tres pueros morti addictos [deditos/at—N] illesos abire fecisti tuis laudibus instantem conserva plebem. Namque cre.

3n, 2r.   3n, 1r—B,E,H,S,Y.   2v, r—E.

Ps.-Romanos, 22 (p. 208): Quo modo praeter spem, homines per somnia eruisti ab ergastulo qui morituri erant, nec nisi ex memoria nomen tuum usurparunt, O magne...

S. Theodoros Studites, 5 (p. 356): Tu vinculis constrictos a morte erupisti saevissima dum terribilis imperatori in somno apparuisti...
6 (p. 356): Canunt enim te abacti juvenes in necem injustam, tres oves tuae...

Cod. Augiensis xxxii (ed. Meisen, p. 529): "Domine Deus sancti Nicolai, exaudi nos, et sicuti salvasti illos tres viros qui in Lycia inique habebantur mori in Myrrim metropoleos, sic et nos salva qui inique et iniuste habemur mori."

Johannes Diaconus (Mombr. 304.20): ... recordatus est qualiter sanctus Nicolaus iuvenum liberator trium mirabilis fuisset... *(305.17–19):* Et nunc, Domine, Domine, miserere nostri, et famuli tui Nicolai intercessione eripe nos ab hac perditione, sicut erepti sunt tres viri illi a pernicioso iugulatu.

37

[XI] LECTIO. Ex multis igitur idolatriis quibus olim [solum—N] prefata regio dedita fuerat maximam dementiae suae devotionem erga nefandissime Dianae simulachrum exhibere studuit, adeo ut etiam usque ad illud servi Dei tempus plerique rusticorum execrabili deservirent [-vunt—N] religioni. Sed vir Dei huius sacrilegii superstitionem non ferens tanta persecutus est instantia ut, divino suffragatus adminiculo, penitus ex illis finibus obsceni numinis culturam propelleret. Verum quid diabolo malitiosius, quod in orbe artificiosius. Cum enim cerneret se privatim tanto decoris sui cultu, fellea face successus, magnam contra Nicholaum exarsit in iram, et novo pectore nova versans consilia. Quosdam adiit viros, omnibus inbutos, imo perditos maleficiis eisque conficere oleum, quod mediacon dicitur, sub omni celeritate precepit. Parent protinus egregii/nefandi* auditores dictis perfidi/cari* magistri, et quantotius portentuosi liquoris mixtionem componunt. Quo confecto haud piger doemon/mox* ad nocendum transformavit se in cuiusdam religiose femine vultum, atque simulata specie quibusdam navigantibus quorum devotio ad servum Dei tendebat, medio sese obtulit mari, quasi aliorum lembo uteretur. Ait eis, "Video quidem vos proficisci ad domnum Nicholaum. Mallem nunc et ego venire vobiscum, quia votum habeo tanti patris perfrui benedictione. Sed quoniam nequeo, rogo vos ut si molestum non est, hoc meae parvitatis oleum ad aecclesiam Myrreorum feratis, ex ob memoria mei summatim exinde parietes ipsius aulae liniatis [lunatis—N]. Illi vero ignari doli artisque fuscatae, sumunt oleum et in classe libenter secum vehunt.

(Mombritius 301.22–41.)

38
R. Sancte Nicholae. V. O Nicholae sidus aureum.

3n, 3r. *Not in other MSS, except* (?): l, r—H.

Ps.-Romanos, 3 (p. 203): Christus enim eum gloria adornavit, mortalibusque dedit magnum sidus omnibus luculentem...
S. Theodoros Studites, 1 (p. 355): In lucida tua vita rutilans ut sol, conspicuus orbi...*3 (p. 256):* Totus orbis, ac si novum sidus effulgeat...

39
[XII] LECTIO. Tunc monstrum informe, velut umbra tenuis veloci evanuit remigio. Sed Dominus pius, invidorum aspernator, non est passus diu simpliciter ad famulum suum properantes munus ferre simulate imaginis, nec sermonibus fantasticis delusos progredi. Ex inproviso enim cernunt sagenulam insignibus refertam hominibus, inter quos conspicantur quendam simillimum sancto Nicholao. Qui ad eos sic facetis interrogationibus

---
* The second element written above the line.

orsus. "Heus," inquit, "quae nam illa mulier vobis locuta est, vel quid vobis attulit?" At illi seriatim cuncta narrantes en aiunt [enaviis—N]. Ostendunt et oleum, "Quod nos deprecata est ad sanctam aecclesiam." Quibus ille, "Vultis evidentius sapere quae fuit femina illa? Haec est enim inpudica Diana. Et ut me pro certo verum dicere comprobetis, hoc vasculum execrandi olei istos [istic—N] projicite [prout te—N] in fluctos [inflictibus —N]." Nulla in medium mora; incunctanter faciunt imperata. Mox autem ubi oleum illud aequoreas tetigit aquas, mirabili dictu, ilico accensus est ignis qui contra naturam oleorum et contra naturam elementi prolixo maris spatio visus est ardere. Haec vero dum nautis stupenda videtur [nautae vident s.—N²] et defixo obtutu herent in tanto prodigio, utrorumque naves magno divisae sunt intervallo. Unde nec interrogare ore valuerunt quis esset ille per quem caledi hostis frustratas agnovere insidias. Verum tamen ut devoverant ad sanctum festinantes Nicholaum clara voce referebant obviantibus sibi quod eis acciderat. Venientes autem ad servum Dei, aiebant, "Vere, tu es ille qui nobis in illo pelago horrendum ostendisti prodigium. Vere, tu verus Dei es famulus ob cuius vitae meritum erepti sumus ab exitialibus diaboli insidiis." Talia dicentes, cunctum rei eventum per ordinem narraverunt. Quibus auditis, vir Domini solito more in laudem prorupit clementissimi Salvatoris, ac deinde admonuit eos iuste et pie vivere, atque se tutele custodis aeterni ex toto committere Qui neminem permittit temptari supra id quod potest. Talibus itaque oraculis satis informatos, optataque benedictione exhilaratos, laetentes homines illos Iesu Christi famulus remisit ad propria.

(Mombritius 301.41–302.7.)

40

R. Celorum rex omnipotens tuam in sancto Nicholao confessore tuo considerantes virtutem tibi totum quod meruit asscribimus. Ideoque precamur ut apud misericordiam [clementiam—N]

The Text

tuam et exemplis eius adiuncemur et meritis. V. Talis quippe nequaquam nisi gratia tua Domine existere valuisset. Ideoque.

3n, 4r. *Not in other MSS.*

41

IN LAUDIBUS

[A] Beatus Nicolaus pontificatus infulis decoratus talem se exhibuit ut ab omnibus amaretur. [*Alter*: Amicus Dei Nicholaus, pontificali decoratus infula, omnibus se amabilem exibuit—Ab, B, E. H, S, Y.]

l, 1a. l, 3a—B,Y. l, 4a—Ab,E,H,S. iv, a—H. p(Dec. 11), a—A. x, a—A. j, cap.—L. (Prosa-sequentia [*saec.* x]—Chevalier, *Repert.* I, 141, No. 2400.)

Johannes Diaconus (Mombr. 299.55): Sicut mos est illius regionis pontificalem accepit infulam. (Cf. *Mombr. 306.16-32*.)

Namur MSS 15 (144.42-43): *Beatus autem Nicolaus pontificatus infula decoratus, talem se exhibuit ut ab omnibus amaretur.*

42

[A] Aecclesiae sanctae frequentatis limina, sacra pectori condebat mandata sagaciter.

l, 2a. j, a—Ab,E,L. l, a(Dec. 11)—A.

Johannes Diaconus (Mombr. 297.44-45): Nunc solus ecclesiarum terebat limina, ... non immemor armariolo pectoris recondebat.

43

A. Infantia teneriori de cursa corpus ieiuniis macerabat. [*Alter*: Beatus Nicholaus adhuc puerulus multo ieiunio macerabat corpus.—Ab, B, E, H, S, V, Y.]

l, 3a. l, 1a—B,E,L,S. h, a—Ab,E,L. v, r—Ab. v, a—A,E. x, a—A.

Johannes Diaconus (Mombr. 297.38-39): Quis enim audit parvulum in die semel et non amplius papilas bibere matris, et facile credit? *(Mombr. 300.12-13)*: Corpus ieiuniis macerabat.

44

A. Iuste et sancte vivendo ad honorem sacerdotii promoveri divinitus.

l, 4a. l, 3a—Ab,B,E,H,S,Y. sext, a—E,H,L. 2v, a—A.

Johannes Diaconus (Mombr. 302.4): Ac deinde monuit eos, iuste et pie vivere.

Cf. Titus ii, 12.

45

A. O per omnia laudabilem virum cuius meritis ab omni clade liberantur qui ex toto corde quaerunt illum.

l, 5a. l, 4a—B. z, a—E,H,L. 2v, a—A.

Johannes Diaconus (Mombr. 305.58–306.1): Quis enim digne potest explicare, qualiter eius meritis promerentibus cecis visus... (*cf. 306.16–32*). (*304.32–34*): Quis umquam eum quaesivit puro corde et non invenit? Quis petivit ab eo misericordiam et non accepit?

Namur MS 15 (p. 146.23–25): ...exhiberet tamen eis suae interventionis praesentiam, qui ubique locorum toto corde quaerebant misericordiam suam.

Paris MS B.N. Lat. 5277 (Cat. Cod. Paris I, 461–2): O Christi mira pietas omni laude prosequenda, qui sui famuli Nicolai merita longe lateque mirabiliter declarat. *O per omnia laudabilem virum cujus meritis ab omni clade liberantur qui ex toto corde quaerunt illum.*

46

IN EVANGELIO. O Christi pietas omni prosequenda laude quae sui famuli Nicholai merita longe lateque declarat. Nam ex tumba eius marmorea oleum manat cunctosque languidos sanat.

l, ga. 2v, a—A,B,E,H,S,V,Y. f, a—Ab. m(ante e)—B. 2v, a(Dec. 13, 14)—A. l, a—L.

See 31, 45 above.

Johannes Diaconus (Mombr. 296.45): O mira Domini pietas, mira clementia... (*304.31*): O clemens pietas Salvatoris; O immensa benignitas Creatoris. (*306.2–3*): Quis inquam tante est facundiae ut facile possit exprimere, qualiter ex marmore tumuli eius sacrum resudat oleum. (*Falconius, p. 126, n, calls attention to this parallel.*)

Namur MS 51 (p. 148.30–35): Nam *ex tumba eius oleum* manat, cujus natura quemadmodum est lucis ministra, sic hujus signa gratia anteactas virtutes illustrat et sequentes comprobat, quia cunctos languidos sanat. O immensa *Christi pietas omni laude prosequenda, quae declarat longe lateque sui famuli merita,* quae sint fidelibus quasi quaedam salutis pignora, ut qui per seipsos promereri non possunt vitae remedia consequantur haec per beati Nicolai patrocinia.

The Text

Paris MS Lat. 5277 (see above): Cui omnipotens Deus tot et tanta beneficia contulit, ut illius laudabile nomen per omnes nationes orbis terrarum quamdiu orbita mundi istius volvitur, semper accipit incrementum. Subnixis ergo precibus eum suppliciter exoremus, ut apud Christum ejus patrociniis adiuvemur.

47–56
AD MISSAM

[Nos. 47–56, the liturgy for the Mass, are not part of the *historia*. There seem to have been propers for the Mass in existence before the year 1000 (cf. Meisen, pp. 174–176; Ebner, *Quellen und Forschungen,* 1896; Leroquais, see Index). My annotations relate only to the manuscripts listed above, none of which gives a full outline of all the commons and propers, but nearly all of which represent the Mass in some way.]

47
[INTROIT] Statuit ei Dominus testamentum.

Eccli. xlv, 30 (Introitus in Com. Confessoris Pont.). See Young, *Drama* II, pp. 348, 351, after Coussemaker, *Dram. Liturg.*, p. 330. It concludes the Fleury *Iconia*.

48
COLLECTA. Deus qui beatum Nicholaum pontificem tuum innumeris decorasti miraculis, tribue nobis ut eius meritis et precibus a gehenne incendiis liberemur. Per.

This *oratio* was said at some point in almost every hour of the proper Office and at other occasions.

49
EPISTOLA. Ecce sacerdos.

Used as a, e, cap., vs., r.   iv—Ab,E,H,L.   f—Ab.   j—H,E.   l—E.   p—L.   x(n,l,p)—A. The *versus* is *Amavit eum Dominus*. *Portiforium*, p. xix (Common for Confessors).

50
GRADUALE. Iuravit Dominus. R.

Grad. Domine prevenisti. Alleluia. vs. Justus germinabat.—A,B,E,L,V; *Portiforium*, pp. xx, xxi (a,r Common for Confessors). Sequencia, Congaudentes exultemus [see F. J. E. Raby, *Christian Latin Poetry*, 1927, pp. 345–346; *Anal. Hymn.* LIV, 95–96; Chevalier, *Repert.* I, 228, No. 3795; usually attrib. to Adam of St. Victor (*ca.* 1150), but he is impossibly late]—A,B,E,L,V.

51
EVANGELIA. Sint lumbi vestri preci narr. [precincti].

Luc. xii.35–40. *Vigilate* (Matt. xxiv.42, xxv.13, xxvi.41; Marc. xiii.35, xiv.38; Luc. xxi.36 ?)—A,B,L; *Portiforium*, pp. xx, xxi. *Homo quidam peregre* (Matt. xxv. 14)—B,E. *Homo quidem nobilis*—V.

52

OFFERTORIUM. Veritas mea. V.

1m, *Inveni*—B.   2m, *Posuisti*—B.   m,x, *Posuisti*—A.

53

SECRETUM. Sanctifica qs. Domine oblata munera, quae in veneratione sancti antistis tui NICHOLAI offeruntur, ut per ei vita nostra inter adversa ubique dirigitur et prospera per Dominum.

SECRETA. Per hostias Domine tuae pietati, in sancti Nicolai confessoris tui atque pontificis commemoratione deferimus, quae illius interventu maiestati tuae ad laudem et fragilitate nostrae sint ad saludem, per Dominum.—C.

54

POSTCOMMUNIO. Sacrificia que sumpsimus Domine pro sollempnitate sancti pontificis NICHOLAI sempiterna nos protectione confirmant. Per.

POSTCMM. Sumentes Domine salutis nostrae subsidium, beati Nicolai confessoris tui atque pontificis interventu, ad vitae aeternae proficiamus augmentum. Per.—C.

55

RESPONSORIUM. Servus Dei Nicholaus auri pondo trium virginum redemit pudorem earumque patris inpudicam remense auro fugavit inopiam. [Versus] Affluens itaque misericordiae visceribus metallo duplicato propulsavit earum infamiam. Earumque.

m, 1r.   3n, 1r—Ab.   3n, 2r—B,E,S,Y.   1n, 4r—H.   v,p—H.

Cf. 7 above.

Johannes Diaconus (Mombr. 297.58–298.8): Quod sanctus Nicolaus reperit...decrevit omnino ex suis abundantiis earum supplere inopiam, ne puellae nobilibus ortae natalibus lupinari macularentur infamia...ut ex uno famelici satietur ingluvies et ex alio virginum redimatur incoestus.

56

R. Magne pater NICHOLAI summo Patri proxime, admiranda que precellis apud eum gratia a commissis nos emundans ne cadamus sustine. [Versus] Iam per terras et per mare fame cele-

The Text

berrime refovendo tribulatos et elevando naufragos. [A commissis.]

m, 2r.   3n, 3r—H,Y.   v, r—A,B. See Chevalier, *Repert.* II, 68, No. 10970.

Cf. *Johannes Diaconus (Mombr. 306.16–32.)*

57

AD VESPERAS. Copiose caritatis NICHOLAE pontifex qui cum Deo gloriaris in celi palatio. Condescende, supplicamus, ad te suspirantibus ut exutos gravi carne pertrahas ad superos.

v, a.   f, a—Ab.   l, a—A,B,E,H,S,V.   x, l, a—A.   l, a(Dec. 13)—A. See Chevalier, *Repert.* I, 232, No. 3864. Concludes the Fleury *Getron.* See below, p. 91.

Additional Notes

The scribe of N fills out the folio (155^v) with an abbreviated statement of the miracle of the myrrh, found in John the Deacon, 20 (Mombritius 306.8–12); Otloh, *Namuricensis,* 16 (*Anal. Boll.* II, p. 148) and *Monacensis,* 27 (*ibid.* XVII, pp. 208–209); and the Addendum to John, 14 (Falconius, p. 126, cols. 1–2). Another addendum in Falconius (19–20, p. 124), giving the same substance, suggests that this legend originated with the Life of Nicholas of Sion: *Distat autem Domus Sanctae Sion, ubi requiescit idem confessor, a moenibus civitatis Myreae, quasi milliaribus tribus, ad orientalem plagam, etc.* The words in all the versions I have cited differ.

Items Appearing Elsewhere, Not in *Nero E 1*

[Oratio] Deus bonitatis auctor et bonorum omnium dispensator: concede propicius ut qui beati Nicholai confessoris tui atque pontificis solemnitatem veneramur: eius patrociniis atque suffragiis maiestatis tue propiciacionem consequamur. Per Christum. iv, p—Ab,E.

Amavit eum Dominus.—*Portiforium,* pp. xix–xxii (a, r Common for Confessors), *passim* in manuscripts.

R. Euge serve bone.—A(9 Mai); *Portiforium,* p. xix (Matt. xxv, 21).

A. Justum deduxit Dominus.—A(l, Dec. 6, Mai 9), L(v and sext), Ab (iv,a), *Portiforium,* p. xix (Sap. x, 10).

Vs. Justus ut palma florebit.—H.E(3n), L(l); *Portiforium,* p. xx (Ps. xci, 13).

A. Ora pro nobis beate Nicolae.—A,E,L,H, etc.

Chapter IV

Relevant Legends of Nicholas

THE ANALOGUES and duplicates noted with the text indicate that the bulk of the cursus was derived, often verbatim, from the *Vita Nicolai* composed by the Neapolitan John the Deacon about the year 880. There is no allusion to a legend in the text which can be traced to any other source. Anrich has established that John's only sources were an anonymous text of the *stratilates* legend and a Life of Nicholas composed by Methodios, who later became Patriarch of Constantinople (d. 847).[1]

All published texts of John's *Vita* contain additions of various sorts. This is also true of all manuscripts that I have seen, but I have not attempted to examine them all. What is important to note is that no liturgical manuscript that I have examined contains either *epitomata* or *historiae* which allude to any legend or other matter lying outside John's authentic text, though hymns and proses quite regularly utilize those later additions. However many more legends there were, either imported from the east or invented in the west—and there were many indeed—they were never represented in the anthems and responses. Not all liturgical manuscripts contain lections, but of those which do the only one, to my knowledge, which goes beyond the text of John is the Hyde Abbey MS (H), which was written *ca.* 1300 and is therefore quite late. The "authentic John" is represented by *Nero E 1*.

Because of the discussion to follow, I list here by catch-phrases eleven legends which are pertinent to the liturgy. For each I record: (*a*) the pages and lines in Mombritius' text, (*b*) page-references to a complete discussion in Meisen's work, (*c*) the numbers of the pertinent sections of the liturgy above, (*d*) a

---

[1] Born in Syracuse, Methodios had a rich and noble father who was saved from shipwreck by Nicholas, whom he invoked as he went beneath the waves (see Eugéne Marin, *Saint Nicolas,* 2 ed., Paris, 1917, p. 147).

Relevant Legends of Nicholas 43

brief statement of the legend, (*e*) data not usually mentioned which have come to my attention.

1. *Parentage.* (*a*) 297.15–24. (*b*) No discussion. (*c*) 4, 27. (*d*) Born of well-to-do, wise, pious parents.

2. *Devout Childhood.* (*a*) 297.24–45. (*b*) P. 259. (*c*) 5, 8, 11, 21, 22, 34, 42, 43. (*d*) From birth Nicholas sucked but once on each Wednesday and Friday. A pious, earnest youth.

3. *Three Daughters,* (*a*) 297.45–299.26 (*b*) Pp. 232–245. (*c*) 6, 7, 55. (*d*) The orphaned young man Nicholas learns that a neighbor, in unwonted poverty, contemplates selling his three daughters to brothels. As each reaches age, Nicholas covertly hurls a bag of gold through the window to save her. (*e*) The German Life of a fictitious St. Suibert of Bethlehem borrows this tale from Nicholas (*Anal. Boll.* LXVI [1948], p. 116).

4. *Chosen Bishop.* (*a*) 299.26–300.7. (*b*) No discussion. (*c*) 2, 3, 9, 10, 12, 13, 14, 16, 18. (*d*) On the death of the bishop of Myra, the council of bishops, inspired, decides to appoint the first man to appear at the church door in the morning. Nicholas is the first. (*d*) The Princeton Index of Christian Art shows this to be one of the most popular of all Nicholas legends in medieval art—an indication that the cult was more clerical than claustral. Such an inference is supported by medieval letters; so, e.g., Nicholas is a primary image in Salimbene's *Liber de praelato.*

5. *Virtues.* (*a*) 300.7–28. (*b*) No discussion. (*c*) 24, 26, 41. (*d*) Grave, humble, eloquent, abstinent, chaste, disciplinary, charitable, censorious of injustice, careful, dignified.

6. *Rescues Sailors.* (*a*) 300.28–43. (*b*) Pp. 245–249. (*c*) 15, 28, 30. (*d*) While Nicholas is still alive, his likeness rescues sailors imperiled by tempest. (*e*) Orderic Vitalis tells of William the Conqueror's being saved from shipwreck by Nicholas. The English Channel became a favorite water for such rescues. For others see, e.g., *Cat. Cod. Paris.* II, 405, 415; another tale, *ibid.,* pp. 427–29, tells of a rescue of crusaders and pilgrims near Cyprus: Nicholas "habebat tam praeclarum vultum et splendi-

dum quasi crystallum mundissimam; habebat et capillos tam candidos quasi lana mundissima et candida, barbam quoque prolixam et candissimam, quae in eo demonstrat magnam reverentiam et auctoritatem. Amictus quoque erat candidissima stola, nec in eo aliquid apparebat nisi candor, sicut res quae tota erat ex Deo." This peculiarly Walloon iconography, which I believe to be exclusive with Nicholas, has persisted in the Lowland Sinterklaes.

7. *Grain-ships.* (*a*) 300.43–301.22. (*b*) Pp. 249–253. (*c*) 19, 33, 35. (*d*) During a famine at Myra, Nicholas persuades the captain of an imperial grain fleet to part with modicums of grain. When the ships reach Byzantium, the grain has miraculously been restored, yet Myra has enough for both food and planting.

8. *Diana.* (*a*) 301.22–302.7. (*b*) Pp. 269–275. (*c*) 37, 39. (*d*) A likeness of Diana persuades mariners going to Myra to carry a phial of oil to Nicholas's church. A likeness of Nicholas appears to the mariners at sea and persuades them to throw the phial overboard. It explodes on contact with the water. (*e*) Diana of the Ephesians was among the deities of sailors (see Lactantius, *Pat. Lat.* VI, 237); *a gehenne incendiis* in the collect No. 48 above alludes to this legend. See Pauly-Wissowa, s.v. *Artemis,* for her cult at Myra, and Anichkof in *Folk-Lore* V (1894), pp. 108–120. On the extirpation of these pagan cults in *saec.* v, see Fliche et Martin, IV, 19–29.

9. *Stratilates.* (*a*) 302.8–305.52. (*b*) Pp. 219–232, 55–56. (*c*) 29, 36. (*d*) Always combined with the next legend (10).

10. *Citizens of Myra.* (*a*) 302.17–303.21. (*b*) As 9. (*c*) 17, 20. (*d*) Three lieutenants (*stratilates*) of emperor Constantine witness Nicholas's saving three citizens (*cives, iuvenes*) of Myra from death by decree of the tyrant of Myra. On their return to Constantinople, the lieutenants in turn are unjustly condemned to death. On their invoking Nicholas a likeness appears to Constantine in his chamber and overrules the decree. (*e*) An analogue which may have been the inspiration for this earliest of Nicholas legends is that of Eutychianus, as recorded by Socrates,

Hist. Eccl. i, 13 (equals Sozomen i, 14). This is the only extant legend to which Theodore the Studite alludes in his hymn, and the only one retained in the reformed Roman Martyrology, which was derived from Wandalbert (*saec.* ix): Myrae, quae est metropolis Lyciae, natalis sancti Nicolai Episcopi et confessoris, de quo inter plura miraculorum insignia illud memorabile fertur, quod Imperatorem Constantinum ab interitu quorumdam se invocantium, longe constitutus, ad misericordiam per visum monitis deflexit, et minis. (*Martyrologium Romanum Gregorii XIII. Pont. Max. iussu editum,* Antwerp: Plantin, 1635, pp. 426-27.) There can be slight question that the Ottonian cult of Nicholas was largely inspired by this legend, for it well fitted the pretensions based on the Donation. The rise in popularity of the history of Thomas of Canterbury may partly account for the decline in popularity of this legend in the west.

11. *Myrrh.* (*a*) 305.53–306.32. (*b*) See Meisen's Index, s.v. *Manna.* (*c*) 23, 25, 31, 32, 38, 40(?), 45, 46, 56, 57. (*d*) From Nicholas's tomb in Myra, a perpetual exuding of healing liquor is collected; his miracles proliferate. (*e*) The manner of collection is described in a tenth-century poem cited by Du Méril, *Poésies,* p. 172:

> Custodes ibi quatuor
> Inventi sunt in atrio
> Qui extrahunt peniculo
> Liquorem more solito.

The progenitor of the *myroblites* apparently is St. Menas. By the fourth century, a pilgrimage to Egypt to secure an ampoule of the liquor from his tomb was established convention; see *DACL,* s.v., "Ampoules" (I, 1722–1747) and "Saint Ménas" (XI, 380–397), and L. Brehier, *Le monde byzantin* III, 265. Demetrios, whose *Vita* was composed for Charles III by Anastasius the librarian (*BHL,* No. 2122), was a renowned myroblite. Such instances are especially centered in and about Cyprus; see *Leontius Makhairas, Recital ... Entitled 'Chronicle,'* ed. R. M.

Dawkins, Oxford, 1932, II, pp. 63-64; Anrich I, 451, etc.; Pio Scognamiglio, O.P., *La Manna de S. Nicola,* Bari (S.T.E.B.), 1925; J. Laroche, "La manna de saint Nicolas," *Revue de la Suisse catholique,* 1890, pp. 56 ff. Grant Loomis, *White Magic,* 1948, p. 43, nn. 87, 89-91, lists 14 such saints without mentioning the three above and hardly duplicating a longer list compiled by Théophile Raynaud, *Opera* VIII (Lyon, 1665), pp. 517-522. The apostles Andrew and Matthew, John the Almoner, Felix of Nola, Eloi, and Médard are others.

Relevant to the discussion here are Catherine of Alexandria, who becomes Nicholas's female counterpart in many ways, Gondechar the bishop of Eichstätt, and Walpurga the sister of Willibald and abbess of Heidenheim in the diocese of Eichstätt. These all seem to have acquired their power from Nicholas. The *Anonymous Haserensis* (Mon. Germ. Hist., *Scriptores* VII, 256) testifies that Reginold's benefactor Pia, prototype of the Bari widow (see below), became a myroblite: "Unde hodieque ex sarcaphago venerabiles eius cineres continente vivae instar aquae, ut oleum de tumba sancti Nicolai, iugiter manat, multosque languidos mira efficacia sanat." (Cf. Response 31, above.) See also Johannes Frey in *Giessener Beiträge zur deutsche Philologie* LXI (1938), p. 90. These German instances seem to result from the popularity of the liturgy; but it also seems clear, from the texts, that the spread of the Nicholas cult was fostered by the ampoules of myrrh which pilgrims obtained in the east (it continued to run after the Translation, both at Myra and at Bari, and still does). So, the monk of Bec, *Vita S. Nicolai (Cat. Cod. Paris.* II, 414), tells of a layman, Isoardus, who secured as a relic "de oleo quod excedat a sacris artubus ejus," and erected an altar in the chapel of St. Mary at Bec to contain it. Meisen, p. 105, quotes pope Clement V, July 26, 1306, encouraging pilgrims to go to "ecclesiam beati Nicolai confessoris Barensis... ad quam propter distillationem liquoris qui ex ipsius gloriosissimi confessoris ossibus, ut pie creditur, incessanter emanat, populorum maximus de diversis mundi partibus sit concursus..."

Chapter V

Legends About the Liturgy

TWO QUITE DISTINCT legends regarding the introduction of the liturgy were evidently composed in northern France or the lowlands. One tells of the introduction of the liturgy into the Cluniac Office, the other of its composition in the city of Bari following the Translation. The two legends have elements in common, and they seem to preserve some kind of poetic truth. Because the Latin texts are accessible, I render them in English, without abridgment.

The first, which exists in two recensions, was published by the Bollandists[1] and reprinted by Coffman.[2] Later, Young again reprinted the second recension.[3] It is this recension which James of Voragine used in his *Golden Legend*.[4] The tale runs as follows:

> Among the countless indications of those powers by which the blessed Nicholas shines among the spiritual fathers with the unique radiance of the morning star,[5] as if in the stellar reaches, it seems proper to include evidence from our own day as well. It will show how he favors his devout servants while being displeased with the detractors from his service. How this actuality came about, I will carefully but briefly describe.
>
> The new *historia* of St. Nicholas' life and miracles was composed, to be sure, by a man, but by a man who was divinely inspired. But even when, because of its overwhelming sweetness, it was being

---

[1] One recension in *Cat. Cod. Paris.*, II, pp. 430–431, from MS *Lat. 5638, saec.* xiv; the second, *ibid.* I, pp. 510–511, from MS *Lat. 5284, saec.* xiii. The editors were not sure which recension was composed first; see II, p. 430. One or both could have been invented in the twelfth century, or, indeed, earlier. In 1941 Coffman said "approximately 1050–1100" (*Renaissance Studies in Honor of Gordon Craig*, p. 14).

[2] *New Theory*, pp. 51–53.

[3] *Manly*, pp. 254–255.

[4] Th. Graesse, ed., *Jacobi a Voragine, Legenda Aurea*, 1846, pp. 841–842. Ch. CLXXXI, which, according to James, was to be a brief history of his own Lombard people, is in fact a chronological arrangement of those events of all western Europe after the sixth century which James considered especially important. The presence of this legend indicates the interest in the topic.

[5] See above Nos. 4, 38.

[47]

devoutly chanted far and wide among the churches of Christ throughout nearly the whole of the Latin world, it had never been instituted in a cell named Cross, subject of St. Mary of Charity,[6] because of the sloth of the inmates. There came a day when the elders of the establishment appeared in a body before Dom Ytherius, that is, their prior, and humbly requested that he permit them to psalm the responses of the blessed Nicholas. Far from acquiescing to their petitions, he replied that it would be totally out of order in this way to change the ancient custom (*morem pristinum*) by any such innovations. While pondering this harsh decision of their father, they began to argue the matter with words of this sort: "Why, father, do you disdain to listen to your sons? Why, when the *historia* of St. Nicholas, full of sweet spiritual honey, is already honored through nearly the whole globe, cannot we chant it? Why cannot we like others be refreshed at such a feast? Do you suffer us to fast before such a spiritually reviving refection? Why, with all the churches committed to jubilation through this new leaven, must this cell alone now remain in mute silence?"

When these and other like queries had sufficiently annoyed the prior, he burst out with blasphemies like these: "Leave, brothers. For I certainly will never give you the right to abandon the ancient rite (*relicto pristino usu*) and to admit new songs of worldly clerks, indeed of a kind of jonglerie (*nova saecularium cantica clericorum, immo jocularia quaedam*), into a church in which I serve at the command of God."

When they heard his words of rejection, they were quite overwhelmed in blushes. Not being able to protest further, the disciples kept their peace, and at the subsequent feast they carried through the evening and morning office (*vespertinam matutinalemque synaxim*) according to custom, though not without some sorrow. Then when the vigils were over, they went to their own beds to sleep.

But when the prior lay down on his cot as did the others, lo, the blessed Nicholas appeared visibly before him with a fearful demeanor and upbraided him in the bitterest terms for his obstinacy and pride. Dragging him from bed by the hair, he shoved him to the floor of

---

[6] B. Maria de Caritate, founded in 706, was given to Cluny in 1059 by Geoffrey, of Auxerre; see Guy de Valous, *L'ordre de Cluny* (Archives de la France monastique, XL), 1935, p. 136. The neumed Bibl. Nat. MS *Lat. 12601,* which Auda (p. 47) says probably originated at Cluny in early *saec.* xi, and thereafter belonged to Saint-Maur-des Fossés, contains the Nicholas liturgy. A letter of Peter the Venerable to the bishop of Liège (*Pat. Lat.* CLXXXIX, 277) makes clear the tradition of exchange between that abbey and the diocese.

Legends About the Liturgy

the dormitory. Beginning the anthem *O pastor aeterne,* and with each modulation inflicting most severe blows on the back of the sufferer with the switches which he held in his hand, he taught the wayward prior to sing the whole from beginning to end.

Hysterical from such blows and from the strange vision, the prior began to cry out unintelligibly, and at the cries the brothers quickly ran together before him. Seeing him alone but prostrate, they sollicitously tried to find out what he had seen or suffered. But he, as if he were beside himself, was not able to give any answer to their inquiries. Lifted up by the hands of the brothers, he was carried to the infirmary, and for some days was in the grip of a profound lethargy. At last, restored by divine compassion and the intervention of the blessed Nicholas, he addressed the brothers in congregation: "Observe, my dearest sons, that after I refused to obey you I underwent severe punishment for my hardness of heart. Now do I not only freely accord with your request, but as long as I live I will be the first and most skillful chanter of the *historia* of that great father."

Note that Nicholas here acts in character with the most ancient legend, *Stratilates*.[7] This kind of appearance for the purpose of administering a flogging is a very common motif in Nicholas legends, but seems uncommon in legends of other saints. The only other example that has come to my attention is German and lies along the path of extension of the Nicholas liturgy. It is told of St. Jude by Caesarius of Heisterbach,[8] in whose abbey an intense cult of Nicholas had developed. A legend of St. Gregory the Great, as related in a *vita* composed in England early in the eighth century but extant only in a manuscript

---

[7] As in a Reichenau manuscript of *saec.* ix, ed. Meisen, pp. 527–530. Raban Maur had abridged this text for his Martyrology (*Pat. Lat.* CX, 1183). In the other recension of the legend of Crux, Nicholas *coepit eum vehementer verberare, more consuetudo magistri puero nolenti discere litteras;* consequently Meisen (pp. 394–95) regarded this tale as the earliest evidence of the modern Germanic Nicholas who calls on Nicholas Eve with switches to chastise errant schoolboys: "In fact, the story has impact only in the milieu of the cloister school." Why *cloister* school? Switching is certainly perennially associated with discipline, especially scholastic discipline. On discipline by ferule at the cathedral of Liège *ca.* 1000, see Kurth, I, pp. 292–295. We may well believe that the switches which appear in *Stratilates* are one element in developing the cult of schoolboys; we shall consider below the history of the schoolboy cult. But because of the fraternal and vocational type of instruction in cloisters, discipline in the classical and diocesan sense was minimal. It is, however, notable that the earliest medieval instances of the switching theme appear to originate in Germany.

[8] *Dialogus Miraculorum* viii, 61.

copied in the ninth century at St. Gall, is somewhat similar. Gregory appeared to his papal successor to remonstrate for actions he considered unfortunate, and inflicted a kick on the head from which the offending pope died.[9] Another analogue is to be found in the story which Ekkehart IV told of Ratpert and Tuotilo of St. Gall, who thrashed the sycophant Sindolf.[10] It has elements of the German humor of the period. As Tuotilo played the avenging angel, so might a monk of Crux have played the part of Nicholas. A final analogue is a legend told by Otloh, as related to him by Wolferius of Hildesheim, which I treat below, pp. 94–95.

In the legend of the Cluniac office the crux of the objection to the Nicholas liturgy lies in *scripta quidem per hominem sed homini divinitus inspirata.*[11] This objection to admitting non-scriptural words into the ritual had always existed. It had impeded the introduction of hymns and, later, the sequences of the jubilations. Now conservatives were objecting to the non-scriptural texts contained in *historiae*. These anthems and responses are not psalms, but man-made, is the prior's contention.

The prior's *usus pristinus* was the Roman rite as developed by Carolingian clergy. King Pippin had imposed the Roman chant, and Charlemagne had enforced it: "Ut cantum romanum pleniter discant, et ordinabiliter per nocturnale vel gradale officium peragatur, secundum quod beatae memoriae genitor noster Pippinus rex decertavit ut fieret..."[12] In interpreting

---

[9] See my *Saints' Lives and Chronicles*, 1947, p. 116.

[10] In the *Casus S. Galli, saec.* xi (Mon. Germ. Hist., *Scriptores* II, pp. 94 ff.; trans. G. G. Coulton, *Life in the Middle Ages* IV, 1930, pp. 52–55).

[11] *Cat. Cod. Paris.*, I, p. 510, line 22.

[12] *Admonitio generalis, anno 789* (Mon. Germ. Hist., *Legum sectio* II, t. I, pp. 60–61). See F. A. Gevaert, *La melopee antique* (1895), p. 183. In the other recension of the Crux legend the prior states, "In vestra ecclesia cantatur cantate, et nil amplius." The Council of Aix, A.D. 816, decreed: "Constituantur interea seniores fratres, probabiliores scilicet vitae, qui tempore statuto vicissim cum cantorum scola sint, ne hi, qui discere debent, aut otio vacant aut inanibus et supervacuis fabulis instent." (Mon. Germ. Hist., *Legum sectio* III, t. II, p. 413; see also Pietzsch, pp. 102–104, 116 ff.). Decrees of bishops and of provincial councils were often phrased as follows: "Ut aliud in ecclesia non legatur aut cantetur, nisi ea quae auctoritatis divinae sunt, et patrum orthodoxorum sanxit auctoritas..." (*Pat. Lat.* CXV, 14).

Legends About the Liturgy

these words we know fairly well what the Mass was like, but the Office remains dark.[13] The *Responsale gregorianum,* which was basically arranged by pope Hadrian (A.D. 784-785) was imported to France in 823 and deposited at Corbie, where it became the foundation for Amalarius' ordering of the liturgy. Hadrian, influenced by Greek innovations, had favored proper chants for some saintly confessors, and Amalarius adapted his Roman rite to Gallican use.[14] St. Martin had, since the days of Sulpicius Severus, held a unique place among the religious of the west, and it is easy to assume that he and St. Remi would be among the first to be specially venerated. Regino of Prüm's canons (*ca.* 900) define the subjects of the *usus pristinus:* "Festos dies in anno celebrare sancimus, id est, diem dominicam Paschae cum omni hebdomada, diem Ascensionis Domini, Pentecosten similiter ut in Pascha, apostolorum Petri et Pauli diem unum, Nativitatem sancti Iohannis Baptistae, Assumptionem sancti Mariae, sancti Michaelis, sancti Remigii, sancti Martini, sancti Andreae, in Natale Domini dies quatuor, octavam Domini, Epiphaniam Domini, Purificationem sancti Mariae; et illas festivitates martyrum vel confessorum observare decrevimus quorum in unaquaque paroechia corpora requiescunt."[15] In the main, fresh creation was limited to hymns and processionals of the Hilarian and Ambrosian tradition.

It has often been assumed that composition of proper offices for postapostolic saints, especially confessors, developed only with the rage for so-called "poetic offices" in the eleventh century and thereafter. Presumptively in the second half of that century some monks modified the tradition of the "Roman rite" by introducing new and extensive compositions of both

---

[13] Willi Apel, *Gregorian Chant,* 1958, pp. 61, 95, remarks that Batiffol's statement of 1898 is still valid: "The critical study of the literature of the Responsories has yet to be undertaken."

[14] Gevaert, pp. 178–188, 423–429. See Dom Morin's statement in *Dict. de théologie catholique,* I, p. 434; he studied Amalarius' liturgical work in a series of articles in *Revue Bénédictine,* VIII–XIII (1891–1896).

[15] *De eccles. discipl.* I, 377 (*Pat. Lat.,* CXXXII, 265). Auda, p. 82, cites a later monk of Prüm, Potho, who protested against admitting new feasts.

melodies and words, especially into the Matins, doubtless violating the religious sensibilities of those who would adhere to scriptural language and traditional melodies—that is, melodies which were believed to have come unaltered from Hebrew and Greek temples. It is now becoming apparent that "uninspired composition," that is, creations of western artists, began quite early, if, indeed, they had not always appeared in some degree.[16] Though Pippin and Charlemagne, whose dominant interest was order and uniformity in a vast realm, frowned on innovation, it developed momentum with Charlemagne's death. Metz, as the greatest choir center of the ninth century, may have led the way; but texts from Metz have not survived. The numerous texts from St. Gall indicate that free composition of propers and tropes was rife there and throughout Upper Germany before the century ended.

Because composition of proper offices of the Nicholas type has not been traced systematically, it will be helpful to arrange the scattered evidence in chronological sequence.

The earliest is an antiphonary from Compiègne (Bibl. Nat. MS, *Lat. 17436*), which Dom Louis Brou believes to have been written for Charles the Bald between 860 and 877. It contains propers for a number of saints of Frankish cult, including Vaast, Médard, Germain of Paris, Denis, Martin, and Quentin. Brou has edited and systematically studied the Office for St. Vaast.[17] Lacunae and a missing sheet prevent our knowing much about the anthems, but the nine responses in prose are derived, often verbatim, from Alcuin's *Life* of the saint. These responses are wholly repeated, with addition of three more for claustral use, in two Arras manuscripts of *saec*. xi that also contain neumes and proper anthems together with a second full office used for the octave; two of the forty-seven anthems are rhymed. If

---

[16] See the excellent statement by Dom Andre Wilmart in *Revue Bénédictine*, LI (1939), pp. 62–63.

[17] *Études grégoriennes*, IV (1961), pp. 7–42. The text of the Compiègne manuscript was first published by the Maurists in *saec*. xviii as part of the complete works of Gregory the Great; reprinted in *Pat. Lat.*, LXXVIII, 725–850.

we conclude with Brou that Charles the Bald gleaned these many offices from a variety of local cults, we see that a tradition of original verbal composition in an ordered pattern of anthems and responses was established in a variety of Frankish cathedrals before A.D. 877. Indeed, Brou rather unconvincingly reasons that an office had been composed for St. Vaast before Alcuin composed his *Life*. The manuscript does not supply evidence of new melodic composition. Nor is there evidence of claustral use of such offices.[18]

In 1923, M. Antoine Auda devoted a long monograph to the contention that bishop Stephen of Liège (901–920) was composer and author of three proper offices: *St. Stephen, Holy Trinity,* and *St. Lambert*.[19] Stephen, of noble birth, was related to the powerful counts Gérard and Matfrid of Lorraine, and Charles the Simple called him cousin.[20] He studied at the palace school of Charles the Bald with two other future bishops, Mention of Chalons and Radbod of Utrecht, and then at the cathedral school at Metz. An able politician, he enriched his subsequent posts. Auda's thesis is at no point indisputable; it reduces itself too largely to unclear testimony of the chronicler Anselm (A.D. 1052–1056). That Stephen composed either the *Vita S. Stephani* or the Office is not firmly established; one or both may have been done by another Stephen, then or thereafter.[21] Of the other two, Solange Corbin says, "Apparently, strong reservations are in order regarding the *Office of Trinity,* and Stephen did not originate the *Office of Saint Lambert* but adapted preexistent material and assonanced pieces in arrang-

---

[18] Despite the activity of Notker and his contemporaries at St. Gall at the end of the century, no *historia* appears among the remains.

[19] See chapter II, note 22. His contention was repeated in brief in his *La musique et les musiciens de l'anciens pays de Liège*, 1930, pp. 17 ff.

[20] É. de Moreau, *Histoire de l'Église en Belgique*, I (2ᵉ ed., 1945), p. 270.

[21] See Auda's *Étienne*, pp. 42 and 52 ff. The first seemingly direct statement is in *Micrologus*, attributed to Bernold of Constance (*saec.* xi^fin), *Pat. Lat.*, CLI, 1019: "Quidam autem officium de Sancta Trinitate in octava Pentecostes instituerunt. Nam quidam Leodicensis Stephanus idem officium, sicut et historiam de Inventione Sancti Stephani, composuisse asseritur; quae utraque ab apostolica sede respuuntur." This statement was then caught up in *Mitrale* (*Pat. Lat.*, CCXIII, 386).

ing that office."[22] In any event the manuscript of the latter, which Auda regarded as contemporary, appears on paleographical evidence to have been written at the end of *saec*. x.

There may be slightly less doubt about Radbod's composition of the *Office of Saint Martin*. Radbod studied with Stephen under Manno in the court of Charles the Bald; he then studied under abbot Hugh of St. Martin's, Tours. The office[23] is very similar in construction to the Nicholas liturgy, except that there are two versified antiphons, one in trochaic septenarius, the other in elegaic. The office is anonymous in the single extant manuscript, of *saec*. xii; the attribution is based on the repeated and unequivocal statement in the *Vita Radbodi,* which was composed at some time between 917 and 1064, when it was used by Adam of Bremen.[24] To accept this attribution we must reject a statement by Guitbert of Gembloux that the office was composed by Adelbald of Utrecht, disciple of Gerbert, *saec*. xi^1.[25]

The Antiphonary of Mont-Renaud, which has been open to study only in this generation, has been reproduced in facsimile in *Paléographie Musicale* XVI (1955). The editor, Dom Joseph Gajard, places the text A.D. 950–955 and the neumes *ca*. 1000; he says that it was designed for the monks of St. Eloi at Noyon. It contains a large number of proper offices for confessors, including such saints of local veneration as Denis and his companions, Quentin, Eloi, Fuscien, and Nicaise.

The Antiphonary of Hartker, St. Gall MS *390–391,* of the end of *saec*. x, has been published in facsimile in *Paléographie Musicale,* IIe sér., i (1900). Availability has determined that most views of this century's critics regarding the development of proper offices have been based on the evidence of this manuscript.

---

[22] *Essai sur la musique religieuse Portugaise au moyen âge (1100–1385),* 1952, pp. 338–339. On the Office of Holy Trinity, which has been widely discussed, see Apel, *Greg. Ch.,* p. 8, n. 6.

[23] Mon. Germ. Hist., *Poetae* IV, pp. 163–165; cf. Manitius I, p. 604, and Auda, *La musique,* p. 25.

[24] *BHL,* No. 7046. The passages appear in *Pat. Lat., CXXXII,* cols. 543 and 546; cf. *Anal. Boll.* VI, pp. 5–15.

[25] Manitius, II, p. 812.

Legends About the Liturgy

It seems clear that by the end of the tenth century composition of proper offices for confessors of local veneration was in full swing.[26] I give but two informative later instances: Sigibert of Gembloux (*ca.* 1030–1112) states that "I wrote the *Life of St. Guibert,* confessor and founder of the church of Gembloux. I have drawn from that Life the Lections which I have arranged in order for the office of the saint. I have composed the chant for the anthems and responses of the offices of St. Macloue and of St. Guibert." Elsewhere he wrote that he "composed the text and noted the music of the anthems and responses for the office of St. Malo." Bruno of Alsace (1002–1054), of noble family, canon and then bishop of Toul, who became pope St. Leo IX, composed responses for the feasts of Gregory the Great, Cyriacus, Hydulphe, Odile, and Gorgon, and hymn chants for Nicholas, Columban, Dié, and Richard.[27]

From such evidence I conclude that proper offices, in general of the type of the Nicholas office, were composed in the Frankish empire and became of strictly secular interest in the palace school of Charles the Bald, whence the art spread among the bishops, especially of Lorraine and the Rhineland. There is no evidence that new melodies were composed in the ninth century, and any evidence of new melodic composition before 960 is beclouded. There is also no evidence before that date of monastic interest in this liturgical practice, though to be sure it is clear that troping and other forms of liturgical embellishment occurred at St. Gall in the second half of the ninth century. It may well be that the continuous Hungarian invasions of Lorraine and the Rhineland from 906 to 954 slowed down the natural development.[28]

To conclude from this manifestly indecisive evidence, the prior of Crux (or the story-teller) appears to represent an ob-

---

[26] See Peter Wagner, *Einführung in die gregorianischen Melodien*, 2 Aufl., pp. 134 and 311, and his "Zu m.a. Offiziums-komposition," *Kirchenmusikalisches Jahrbuch*, XXI (1908), in which he outlines the historia of St. Caecilia from Hartker's manuscript.

[27] Amédée Gastoué, *L'art grégorien*, 1911, pp. 89–90.

[28] Louis Halphen, *Les barbares*, 5ᵉ ed. (1948), pp. 334–345, with bibliography.

jection to innovation which centered in France rather than Lorraine and Germany, and in monasteries rather than among the secular clergy. Moreover, the objection to introduction of the Nicholas liturgy seems to have been based on the worldliness of the cult, on the absence of all scriptural verbalism in the texts, and, above all, on the novelty of the melodies. *Cantatur cantate et nil amplius,* if I interpret aright, states that only traditional melodies were acceptable.[29]

At this distance one can tell no more about the tone of the words than of the music. *Nova saecularium cantica clericorum* points to the secular clergy of the rising diocesan schools, regarded by the monks as light-minded and given to frivolities, *immo jocularia quaedam.* We cannot recover double entendres, but that students in external schools cultivated them regularly there is abundant evidence. *Nova cantica* suggests Response 34, *O nova res,* and *futurum amatorem* may be an instance of secular overtones from clerks now turning to Ovid. The prior, well chastened by Nicholas' whip, next day *per ordinem* morose canendo *ad finem usque perduxit.* If there were wordplays in the texts, the prior could not enjoy them even after chastisement. The brothers pleaded only the honied sweetness of the lyrics, a phrase used also to justify troubador verses at later date. At all events, the story of Crux appears to have been coined to justify the introduction of a questionable, worldly liturgy into the service of a militantly reformed order.

The second legend, though also published by the Bollandists,[30]

---

[29] Bernard of Clairvaux, *Epist. cccxcviii,* expresses what had been the Cluniac ideal: "Let the chant be grave, smacking neither of softness nor of rudeness, suave without being flippant, charming the ear in order to move the heart. It is a most serious injury to piety when it is prevented by the frivolity of the chant..." The early Cluniac customs are represented by the *disciplina Farfarensis,* ed. Dom Bruno Albers, *Consuetudines Monasticae,* I (1900), and by two other texts in Vol. II (1905)—all written before the year 1050. But the Cluniacs were fast responding to the pressures of the times; see Batiffol's *History of the Roman Breviary,* trans. Bayley, 1898, pp. 198–201, for a parallel legend. A brief exposition of the Cluniac hours is that of David Knowles, "The Monastic Horarium," *Downside Review,* LI (1933), pp. 711 ff.

[30] *Cat. Cod. Brux.,* I (1886), pp. 320–322, from the Brussels Royal Library MS 1960–62 (*saec.* xiii), fos. 63ᵛ–66ᵛ. It is one of the numerous addenda to the *Vita S. Nicolai* of John the Deacon to be found in that codex.

Legends About the Liturgy

has had scant attention.[31] It is written in the Ovidian mode of scholars of the twelfth century. In the absence of name, date, and place,[32] it is easiest to imagine a contemporary of the Archpoet or of Walter of Chatillon[33] as composer of this out-of-school exercise. The Bari setting indicates only that the story was composed after 1087 but before the Translation had ceased to be the talk of western Europe. It was common enough for the scholastic story-tellers to choose a *mise-en-place* far from home. Both the provenience of the manuscript and the vague reflections of manners suggest that the author was transalpine.

> *By what man and because of what woman and when the* historia *and* prosa *which is* [sic] *sung of St. Nicholas was composed.*

There was a man of noble birth and handsome features who breathed forth the sum of Helicon in both verse and meter. In the city of Bari, to which the blessed Nicholas had been translated, this man ran a school in those first years after the Translation, when laments for the loss of Nicholas had as yet scarcely dwindled in Myra and the signs of dolor were dissipating in thin air, like wisps of smoke after a funeral pyre.

In that same city lived a widow preeminently endowed in mind, though even richer in wealth and loveliness. In either grace she was so surpassing that by a look she could have enticed a stony Demosthenes to the nuptial bed or have aroused passion in the most chaste Lucrece. But since she was both honest and true, she feared God and venerated all the saints with profound piety. Yet principally did she turn all her love to blessed Nicholas; and that she might preserve that treasure of holy love from rust and moth and flames, she frequently held precious vigils before the tomb of the beloved corpse. Joy in that rich treasure would have remained spotless and unseamed, save that the beauty of her soul was sheathed in an alluring body, and against the riches of her mind her earthly wealth contended.

---

[31] Coffman treats it slightly, *New Theory*, p. 58, n. 62.

[32] Aside from the extensive collection of Nicholas legends, the codex contains only sermons for Nicholas Day by Gillebart de Hoiland (d. 1172).

[33] Walter composed the hymn for Nicholas Day inc. *Adest dies annus Nicolai presulis...*, which is No. 11, ed. Karl Strecker, *Die Gedichte Walters von Chatillon*, 1925, pp. 16–17. The legends referred to in the hymn lie wholly within the data of the liturgy.

The latter, with its promise of sensual pleasure, might rend her, though it could never strike her down.

The aforesaid youth saw her and was stricken to the marrow. Returning home, on his couch he plotted evil and chose an unrighteous path. And, as is the curse of that disease, he would at one moment in self-accusation execrate his imperiled soul for its tempestuous waywardness, and the next moment recall it from self-banishment to the cauldron of an anguished heart, with tears and punctuating sighs. Woe enveloped him, and tumult of mind: it urged him to confession of his tide of love; then decency and despair recalled him to concealing his desires. Yet, the more he smothered it, the more the fire exploded. Back and forth he warred with himself, but remained enmeshed in his sinfulness. Here is that *amor*, famed in every page of the poets, worthy of scorn, to be sure, lawless and merciless. It scorches its victim, yet presents a glozing front. Thus the wind sinks the bark by gusts which a steady force would have brought to port. Indeed, the vicious mind transforms the countenance, and as the face loses its refinement, the latent corruption is expressed. It is chained to its error, and itself betrays what it lusts for.

The widow called the youth apart and asked what the trouble was; and, very artfully contemplating his silence, she came to understand his tears and revealing sighs. She gently reprimanded him, and firmly said him nay. But time and again he as firmly pursued his rebuffer. By prayers and gifts he begged familiars of the lady to have her servants lead him to her, vainly attempting to draw Venus from the breast of Pallas. But she, evading all the lover's traps, in no wise allowed herself to be drawn into his sensuality: what she regularly denied him, she denied unequivocally. So the youth, unable to shake off a hope forlorn, lapsed into an actual apathy and was for a long time wasted by the double affliction. In the end he roused himself and bridled his feverish love. Though the noble matron had long been annoyed, she now rested easy, safe from threat.

But it happened on the feast of the blessed Nicholas, when according to her solemn custom she was banqueting with her friends, that the talk among the party turned almost wholly and at length to the miracles of that confessor. She held that the clerks of that metropolis should be heartily ashamed that they had not themselves composed a single responsory or prose suitable for praise of that good friend of God or even a canticle by which his venerable feast could joyfully (*jocundius*) be celebrated. Her remark was spread about and conveyed to the languishing clerk just as it had been spoken.

Legends About the Liturgy

Now he was thoroughly versed in the whole art of music, both melody and rhythm. Hope of her favor therefore directed him; his spirit revived in hope, and from joy of mind his whole flesh tingled. The hope of success was for him, as for so many others, medicine. So he arose, leaving his morbid torpor on the bed. Within a few days, his strength restored, he entered the home of his loved one with a large group of his fellows. After greetings and welcome, as they seated themselves they repeated the words of some of the canticles which he had composed in honor of glorious Nicholas. And the lady promised any gift to the one who should complete them, if he should do it well.

Strengthened by her pledge to him, the young man set to work without delay. He returned to his house and, summoning up within him the whole inspiration of poets and prophets, he set to music in neumes and rhythm that prose which begins *Congaudentes* and the response *Confessor Dei Nicolaus*. Indeed, there is such hope which shines through that work, such love, such exaltation in the words, there and throughout, as only the most skillful could express. Yet we had better believe that the Lord Himself, who on other occasions has revealed Truth through the words of false prophets, now for reasons of His own sang the praise of His cherished Nicholas and His glory through the mouth of this sinner. The new work was committed to the examination of many prudent men and adjudged as brilliant as pure gold straight from the furnace.

The oft-mentioned matron was now convinced that there was nothing sung on saints' days more artistic in verse or sweet in sound than this work. Consequently she happily joined in the compliments paid him and rejoiced indeed that now her every desire had been satisfied. Then she asked her poet to name his reward. With the animation of one restored from the dead, he declaimed that the fires in his breast burned with the destructive force of Etna, and without hesitation demanded that one thing alone which he had properly and constantly been denied; for his disgraceful request had in itself the clear reason for its denial. Then she, recalling her ambiguous pledge and suddenly realizing what she had committed herself to, deplored the price of her delusory promise with tears such as they say Phoebus shed at his hasty judgment in the vengeful and total cremation of Phaeton. She besought him to let her alter her word, accepting as his reward whatever wealth she possessed. But neither tears nor promise of riches nor even God could deflect him from his purpose: forgetful of heaven and earth, the blind man pursued his blind error to transgression, placing desire above reason on all counts. He pressed his proposal, asking for this, resolutely hoping for that—the way that children beg their mothers for the moon with weeping and wailing and are not even restrained by a whipping. How true the learned tales that depict Cupid as blind and as a boy![34] And so he steadily insisted on his evil desire, while she fended off the evil hour with modest resistance. She mourned that she was so ensnared; though she could not escape, she tried to dodge. As if oppression might be eased by delay, she acknowledged her promises that she would be his, but begged that she be granted a truce of a day until she could restore to its now long forgotten uses the now disused bedroom, and could with more secrecy arrange for what dared not be observed. She implored this not with womanish but with dutiful tears, words, and glance, by any one of which she could have softened the Sicilian tyrant; yet by all of them she could scarce hold him off until the appointed hour.

Having thereby obtained that little respite, she sat all the day in hairshirt and ashes; then she turned her whole concentration to him who was created refuge for her grace and for us: on the subsequent night she prostrated herself before the tomb of her hope, that is to say, of the blessed Nicholas. By the benign mercy of God, even before she prayed she was heard, for, herself righteous, she but besought righteousness. Yet not knowing that she would have been saved, she dissolved her anguish in words broken with sobs and seasoned her pious petitions with the sweet savor acceptable to God. Indeed, she forgot that she should pray to God, Who had already heard, and to that fountain of mercy, His mother. Instead, he whom They held within their enveloping essence was wholly and completely on her lips—Nicholas: that name is sweet to her above all others; that name which she had repeated a thousand times over she now repeats beseechingly; that name is the beginning and end of each sob; that name before all others is drawn from her fevered brain by her sighs.

And so, swiftly, the good Nicholas, ever indefatigible in response to good vows and the suffrages of his devotees, stood at the bed of the clerk in his episcopal garb. He found the clerk awake and cursing the night's delay with many a sigh; for a night is long to those whom a mistress has promised the following night. She was wakeful in the hope of avoiding shame, he that he might create it; she wept

---

[34] For another use of this scholastic topos, see Walter Map's *De Nugis Curialium* II, xii (ed. Th. Wright, p. 80).

Legends About the Liturgy 61

for fear that she commit weepful acts, he sighed that he might give himself up to sighs.

But in the end iniquity was vanquished by justice, as is ever the result of such warfare—wisdom wins out over folly. Not tolerating so unfair a conflict either to hang long in the balance or to become an unkind victory, blessed Nicholas seized the youth by the hair and held him aloft, then dropped him with a thud. Harshly he chastized the man's sinfulness with the whip which he carried—yet not mercilessly, for he kept himself within bounds of the fright of his victim. Now chastened and wretched, the youth could scarce raise his tearful eyes and blood-drained visage; with frightened and whispered voice, he begged forgiveness, asking how he had transgressed and who his visitor was. (For the saint of the Lord and his majestic appearance struck terror; and though his whole countenance glowed with compassion, he yet said nothing kindly or affectionate, so that his silence added the more to the stupefaction, while he had vengeance written in his eyes and whole face.) That wretch, but blessed in his very wretchedness, rolled back his eyes as if sunstruck, and prone on the ground tearfully exclaimed with the publican: "Lord, have mercy on me, a sinner." At this the glorious man of the Lord: "I am he, Nicholas, whom you honor with your lips, though your heart be against me, since you have subverted your words to concupiscence. But daughter Jude[35] has sustained not your iniquity. Your evil intents have ensnared her; to her great sorrow mingled with tears, your deceit granted nothing. Now come to your senses and correct every act, that these floggings may cease; and by my intercession you may have that reward for your masterpiece from Him from Whom you have received the gift of composition, Who alone grants and repays such gifts." At these words Nicholas disappeared.

Quickly the chastened youth arose, and hastened to the tomb of his castigator. There he found her at vigils whom for his own pleasure he had rashly lusted after. Casting himself at her feet, he told her what had transpired, and begged her forgiveness and intercession with the blessed saint.

Awestruck by the miracle and with more joy at release from the snare than she had ever experienced before, she exulted and drenched

---

[35] The Altaich legend of a Bavarian Judith (*Acta SS Bollandista*, XXVII, Jun. vii, d. xxix, pp. 455-456) treats of a rich and pious widow in the image of the scriptural Judith. Godehard (see below) was abbot at Altaich. A letter of abbot Eberhard I of Tegernsee (d. 1003), *Ad Juditham, illustrem foeminam, quam rogat, ut afflictae valitudini suae medicinam consulere ne gravetur* is reported in Pez, *Thesaur. Anecd.* V, i, 135-141.

the whole font of her eyes in tears. Then when they had resolved all matters between them and made their peace, saying their prayers and hymns of all kinds, each returned to his home. Thereafter more inclined toward the rites of the precious confessor, they lived out their lives in devotion to him. Thus that always venerable and everywhere hero of God was made the subject and noble refuge of his handmaiden and the sorrow and solace, the wound and the ointment, the bandit and the Samaritan, of the errant clerk.[36]

---

[36] The Monk of Bec (*Cat. Cod. Paris.*, II, pp. 423–424, sect. 29) tells of an adolescent, commended to Nicholas as a baby, who became ensnared by a certain *muliercula*. Advised to leave home and country, he prayed to Nicholas throughout the night, and suffered no further inquietude.

CHAPTER VI

Authorship of the Liturgy

THE AUTHOR of the second legend has combined two themes. The major theme, of the clerk and the lady, I shall treat later. The second theme, of the Nicholas liturgy, parallel with the legend of Crux, is now merely used as a basis for a literary exercise. The objections to the Nicholas liturgy seem to have disappeared, and it is now *a la mode*. This medieval Troilus, the Bari clerk, appeared earlier, as we shall see, than Benoit de Saint-Maur, let alone Chaucer. He is a recognizable forerunner of a French clerk, devotee of St. Nicholas, who loved the daughter of a rich burger.[1] In such fashion did the romantic chaplains develop their courtly idiom while still limited to pious subjects.

Common elements in the two tales, of Crux and of Bari, suggest that the Nicholas liturgy originated in cathedral, not cloister, that conservatives regarded it as frivolous and impious, and that its acceptance was far-reaching and worthy of special attention. Both tales accent its divine inspiration, and its instantaneous acceptance by the discerning when it had a hearing.

Of more specific importance are the initia mentioned; for though they differ in both tales and both recensions of the first tale, all but one are initia of the Nero manuscript and of all other manuscripts which I have compared. The exception is *Congaudentes,* which is the sequence of the gradual of the mass.[2]

---

[1] Strophes 107-123 of the *Vie de Saint Nicolas,* ed. Bohnstedt, from a manuscript (*saec*. xiv) now in the Bibliothèque Nationale.

[2] See above, No. 50. This is Chevalier's No. 3795 (*Repert*. I, p. 228), the normal sequence for the Nicholas Mass, ed. *Anal. Hymn.,* LIV, pp. 95-96, and Mone, III, pp. 455-456 (No. 1093), from manuscripts of *saec*. xi and later. Also F. J. E. Raby, *Christian Latin Poetry,* 1927, pp. 345-346, and *Oxford Book of Med. Lat. Verse* (1959), No. 116, pp. 159-161. It is composed in the syllabically parallel form of the Notkerian sequences, but with strophes terminating in *-a.* The diction leaves no reasonable doubt that it was composed directly from the liturgy of the Nero manuscript: for instance, *Auro per eum virginum tollitur infamia atque patris earundem levatur inopia* (strophe 10; compare anthem 7 above); and so throughout.

It does not appear in Nero, though that manuscript gives the proper texts for the mass; but it is regularly given in manuscripts of the twelfth century. The common attribution of authorship to Adam of St. Victor is therefore impossible. But it does seem possible that the sequence was not in wide circulation before 1060, or it would have appeared in Nero. Raby praises its occasional "great beauty" and speaks of its "transitional style," but does not define his term. The strophes are arranged in isosyllabic doublets in a linear pattern which is basically septenarius, but varied. Each line rhymes with its doublet. This pattern is a development of the German sequence pattern as formulated by Notker. In the absence of more definite evidence, we may best consider it as the composition of a German or one practiced in the Germanic art of composition. A sequence is, by definition, a prose. It is therefore clear that the prose referred to in the rubric of the Bari tale is *Congaudentes,* and that the response *Confessor Dei Nicolaus* exemplifies the *historia* of the rubric.

The initia make clear that these two legends refer to the same liturgy. I have found no second liturgy, and we may be reasonably certain that none ever existed.[3] In the reforms of the sixteenth and seventeenth centuries, it was this liturgy which was deposed.[4]

Let us disregard the Mass and center upon the Office. Who

---

[3] There is, of course, no allusion to Nicholas in the Gelasian or Gregorian sacramentaries; nor is he mentioned by Amalarius of Metz (see Hanssens). Alcuin's litany (*Pat. Lat.,* CI, 522–523) specifies 12 apostles, 12 martyrs, 14 confessors, 11 virgins; but not Nicholas. The list (cols. 591–596) of 600 names of saints (including patriarchs) is intended to be exhaustive; but Nicholas is not named.

[4] See Dom Suitbert Bäumer, *Histoire du Bréviaire,* trans. Biron, II, Paris, 1905. The Commission, sitting 16 May, 1591 (Bäumer II, p. 265) corrected the Nicholas lections; sitting 30 May and 6 and 21 June (II, pp. 265–67), it made further revisions. The last of this office was not removed from Rouen until the reform of 1728; see Collette, p. 287. There is, to be sure, a completely versified, rhymed office, published in *Anal. Hymn.,* XLV[a], pp. 160–163, but it is wholly unrelated to this discussion. Its content, including some very late legends, indicates that it could not well have been composed before the beginning of the fifteenth century. The editors transcribed it from a manuscript of the sixteenth century which came from a French Cistercian cloister. They gave no indication that another manuscript exists. I have not treated it, for it appears to have had no measurable influence and is not related to the topic.

composed it? Meisen[5] represents the majority of recent scholars, including such liturgists as Lambot, Gastoué, Legris, Auda, and Corbin, who identify Isembert, monk of St. Ouen in Rouen, as composing it *ca.* 1030. His only authority is Collette, who so asserted in the year 1902.[6] Meisen at this point followed Collette less critically than was his custom, possibly because the statement so generally accorded with his presumption that the Normans were the agents who popularized the Nicholas cult.[7] Meisen followed up his statements with a list[8] of eight appearances of the rite in Normandy and environs (actually extending to Paris and Chartres) during *saec.* xi, and over sixty places of appearance thereafter.[9] But he drew his data exclusively from Leroquais,[10] whose evidence was largely limited to those regions. Censuses from other parts of Europe would almost certainly have yielded similar results.[11]

Collette, though elsewhere regularly documenting his statements, in this instance cited no source; he wrote:[12]

---

[5] Pp. 176–177.

[6] Collette, p. 64. Henri Leclercq, who accepted Collette's words, even to the extent of transcribing them without quotation marks (*Dictionnaire d'archéologie chrétienne et de liturgie,* IX, 2 (1930), col. 1681), has possibly been most responsible for the acceptance of Collette's assertion as fact.

[7] Certainly the cult was well known at Rouen in Isembert's time. Richard II of Normandy received annually at his court monks from Mount Sinai to whom he paid alms. Richard III in 1028 sent his young son, Nicholas, to Saint-Ouen for education (Guillaume de Jumièges vi, 2, *Pat. Lat.,* CXLIX, 834; cf. Émile Lesne, *Histoire de la propriété eccl. en France* V (1940), p. 115). This Nicholas reigned as abbot of the abbey for nearly 50 years, dying in 1092. His epitaph: "Hic jacet Nicolaus abbas hujus coenobii filius Richardi comitis Normaniae junioris, et frater Roberti comitis, qui rediens ex Hierosolymis apud Niceam urbem mortuus est et sepultus. Hic autem Nicolaus coenobium istud quinquaginta annis rexit prior noster eximius. Obiit autem anno Incarnationis Dominicae 1092, iii Cal. Martis." (*Gallia Christiana,* XI (1874), col. 141D). Nicholas completed the foundations of the present abbey church (col. 136c).

[8] P. 178.

[9] Pp. 178–180.

[10] Leroquais, *Brév.* (see Index); also his *Les sacrametaires et les missels manuscrits des bibl. publiques de France,* 3 vols., Paris, 1924.

[11] Silvestre, in presenting *his* list, judiciously remarked: "A propos de cette liste de mss dans laquelle les documents français sont en majorité, je tiens à mettre le lecteur en garde contre la tendance qu'il aurait de restreindre presque uniquement à la France l'aire de dispersion de l'office en question de S. Nicolas; l'abondance des bréviaires et antiphonaires français provient tout simplement de ce que l'enquête s'est principalement porté sur ce pays." (*Ephemerides Liturgicae* LXVIII (1953), p. 140, n. 7).

[12] P. 64. Since the invention of printing there have been a number of provincial printings of the Nicholas Office, including the Rouennais use; see Chevalier's index to *Repert.,* VI, pp. 164–165. But I have been unable to secure examples.

Isembert, moine de Saint-Ouen, et plus tard abbé du mont Sainte-Catherine, écrit le texte et la musique de l'office de saint Ouen, et de celui de saint Nicholas, non moins célèbre que l'Office de sainte Catherine, composé par Ainard, abbé de ce même monastère. Adoptés tous deux par la plupart des églises, ils devaient servir de modèles pour beaucoup d'autres ..."[13]

Collette was writing the sentence to explain the notable flair for expanding the office by addition of "triple feasts,"[14] with extensive compositions honoring patrons. Collette twice repeated his assertion[15] without evidence, saying that the prose, *Sospitati,* was later added to Isembert's text.

Collette's weaknesses in this section of his book are suggested by his mistaken statement that Ainard was abbot of Sainte-Catherine. According to the records assembled in *Gallia Christiana,*[16] the countess Lescelina asked abbot Isembert for an abbot for her new monastery of St. Peter at Dives, and he finally consented to part with "quemdam de suis magnae auctoritatis virum et nominis, divinis et humanis apprime studiis eruditum, cui Ainardus vocabulum erat, qui quidem genere Teutonicus, sed omni sapientiae disciplina erat morumque pariter honestate praeclarus." Ainard was a spiritual son of Isembert, and they were both Teutonic scholars who, on coming to Normandy, created a sensation. Isembert is described[17] as "natione Teutonicus...rhythmo lugubri parentavit quidam illius temporis monachus a quo vocatur rivus sapientium, patriae consilium, cleri decus ac monachorum singulare speculum." This was Mabillon's digest of the records. Three wards of Isembert, Durand of Troarn, Gerbert of Fontenelle,[18] and Ainard, were hailed by Orderic Vitalis as *tres stellae radiantes,* and especially Ainard:

---

[13] Coffman, *New Theory,* p. 37, in quoting this statement, implied that he was merely summarizing an extensive proof, but this is all. Otto Albrecht, *Four Latin Plays of St. Nicholas,* 1935, p. 15, relied on Coffman.

[14] December 6 was a triple feast at Rouen, and May 9 (Translation) was a *fête du troisième répons double;* for explanation, see Collette, p. 158.

[15] Pp. 147–148, 306.

[16] XI (1874), Instr. 154E (A.D. 1046).

[17] *Ibid.,* cols. 125–126.

[18] Isembert consecrated that new foundation in 1033; see cols. 728–730.

"Gemina scientia pleniter imbutum, versificandi et modulandi cantusque suaves edendi peritissimum. Hoc evidenter probari potest in historiis Kiliani Wirtzieburgensis episcopi,[19] et Catharinae virginis aliisque plurimis cantibus, quos eleganter idem edidit in laudem Creatoris." The reference to Kilian suggests Ainard's homeland as Würzburg before he migrated; we may assume that his master's home was also Franconia. The quality of the musical compositions of both excited Normandy.

The undisguised purpose of Collette, who was a canon of Rouen, in composing his valuable monograph, was to enlist support for restoring to the reformed rite of the Rouen Church some of the medieval art which had disappeared.[20] Rouen has reason to take pride in the sudden development, rich in compositions which spread through Europe.

Beyond a doubt Collette based his undocumented assertions upon statements of Dom Joseph Pothier. That revered liturgist is the source for all attribution to Isembert. In 1895 he published a short article, "Antienne en l'honneur de saint Nicolas" in the *Revue de chant grégorien* III. 10, pp. 147-149; in it he discussed the text and notation of the anthem *O Christi pietas* (No. 46 above) as the source of St. Thomas Aquinas' *O quam suavis es* of the Office of Corpus Christi.[21] He said nothing there about Rouen or Isembert. But in the same journal in 1896 (pp. 49-54), while discussing the "Répons *Virgo flagellatur* de l'office de sainte Catherine," he wrote:

C'est d'abord a la Trinité du Mont Sainte-Catherine, Isembert, son premier abbé, le maitre d'Ainard et de Durand. Moine de Saint-Ouen, il avait composé en l'honneur du patron de son monastère,

---

[19] There is no reference to this work in *BHL* (see Nos. 4660-4663). Evidently it was on the model of the Nicholas *historia*.

[20] See pp. 287, 306. "Au xie siècle, il y a en Normandie toute une pléiade de moines, musiciens et littérateurs, qui enrichessent la liturgie d'offices, dont l'usage se conservera, en partie, jusqu'au xviiie siècle."

[21] See also Corbin, *op. cit.*, pp. 342-343, and A. Gastoué, *L'art grégorien,* 1911, pp. 89-90. Mlle. Corbin, *L'église à la conquête de sa musique,* Paris, 1960, p. 247, states that the music of this song originated in Spanish ritual no later than *saec.* x. I do not know the evidence for her assertion, but some reconciliation with the data I present here would seem to be called for.

avant de le quitter, un office propre, texte et musique. D'après le *Chronicon triplex et unum* (Bibl. de Rouen, cod. Y, 124), il serait également l'auteur du célèbre office de Saint-Nicholas...

In 1897 he repeated the attribution.[22] I have not been able to consult the manuscript in question, but it seems unnecessary to do so. To credit this very late (*saec.* xvii) chronicle where Orderic, who wrote in detail of Rouenais liturgy and was himself a devotee of St. Nicholas, was silent is wishful. But no doubt Dom Pothier unwittingly extended the words of his source.

With the liturgy before us we can understand how the false attribution arose in stages. It began with a statement—which may be true—that Isembert composed the prose for *Ex eius tumba*. The prose *Sospitati,* which does not appear in *Nero E 1,* was an addition to the anthem *Ex eius tumba* (No. 31) in our text; it acquired wide currency.[23] The anthem *O Christi pietas* (No. 46) contains the phrase *ex tumba eius* and duplicates the thought of No. 31. What seems certainly to have happened is that in a successive series of careless steps the authorship of a single composition, *Sospitati,* was extended to three.[24] Isembert may well have been the composer of *Sospitati*. Time, place, and circumstance seem to accord. Since *Sospitati* is clearly an addition to the original office, if Isembert was its composer he was not the composer of the office.

Dom Wilmart, whose mastery of data relevant to such questions is well-nigh impeccable, had already arrived at this conclusion: "D'ailleurs, l'attribution proposée est due simplement au *Chronicon triplex et unum* de Saint-Ouen de Rouen, laquel date du xviie siècle (manuscrit *1201* de la bibliothèque de Rouen); Mabillon s'est bien gardé de lui donner crédit." Hubert

---

[22] *Mémoires sur le musique sacrée en Normandie.* 41 pp.

[23] Published by Dreves and Blume, *Anal. Hymn.* XL, p. 258; Mone (No. 1102), vol. III, p. 464; Young, *Manly,* p. 263; and elsewhere. It is No. 19244 in Chevalier's *Repert.* II, p. 588; cf. No. 40989 (IV, p. 325). Chevalier lists some forty manuscripts, but none of early date.

[24] Chevalier, *ibid.,* was evidently partly aware of this confusion; for, though generally following Pothier, he credited Isembert only with *Ex eius tumba;* see also his *Bibliothèque liturgique,* XIV (Inst. Massil. xiii, 5), p. 14.

Authorship of the Liturgy

Silvestre, who scrutinized the statements of Collette and Meisen with his customary care, could find no warrant for attributing the liturgy to Isembert: "On ne voit pas très bien sur quoi elle repose."[25]

Silvestre suggested that anyone interested had better look in another direction—to a statement of the eleventh-century historian of the diocese of Eichstätt[26] that Reginold, future bishop of Eichstätt (966–991), had composed a *historia* of Nicholas which was immediately so popular that he received his episcopal appointment in consequence.

This statement, which has been cited often enough, has nevertheless been neglected, I believe for two reasons: First, all who have dealt with this topic prejudged the influence of the Normans and centered their eyes on the years about the Translation. Second, there has existed a confusion about the meaning of the word *historia,* which has regularly been used by the medieval writers I have been citing. Indeed, the Bollandists[27] and others only slightly less adept have to this day regarded Reginold's composition as a *vita,* and have so listed it in all reference books, even though no extant *vita* has been identified.[28]

The author of the so-called *Anonymus Haserensis,* written *ca.* 1060, was an abbot in the diocese. He wrote:

Reginold was of noble blood, but even nobler in learning—not alone in Latin and Greek literature, but even somewhat trained in Hebrew; and, what was unique and exceptional indeed, he was the finest musician of his day. *Hic inprimis historiam sancti Nicolai fecit, et pro hoc episcopalem dignitatem promeruit.* Once bishop, with profound study and ardent devotion he composed *historica carmina*

---

[25] *Ephemerides Liturgicae,* LXVII (1953), p. 141.

[26] L. C. Bethmann, ed., "Anonymus Haserensis de Episcopis Eichstatensibus," Mon. Germ. Hist., *Scriptores* VII, pp. 257–258. The passage is reprinted in *Pat. Lat.,* CXLVI, 1011–1012.

[27] *BHL,* No. 6127 (vol. II, p. 291). However, the *Vita* in Namur MS *15,* which will be discussed below, has also sometimes been ascribed to Reginold because of the Bollandists' remark in their catalogue description (*Anal. Boll.,* I, 1882, p. 501): *Auctore, ut videtur, Reginoldo Eichstettensi*—a remark which they later corrected (in *BHL*).

[28] Meisen, pp. 77–79, reviewed the textual evidence and concluded that Reginold, in addition to writing a *vita,* may have composed a hymn.

for St. Willibald, founder and patron of the see. He exerted all his powers of intellect to attain a remarkably varied ornamentation, for he adjoined phrases (*notulas*) at the end of some of the longest responses, and under those phrases he wrote short verses in the fashion of sequences. He did this for the third, sixth, and ninth responses, giving to the third a very few short verses, to the sixth more, and to the ninth many. Now note the arrangement! For the third he added only a little journey, that is, the beginning of pilgrimage, just as Willibald left home; for the sixth, a major, in which he came to Ionia; for the ninth, a very extensive, in which he tried to express the nature of the passage to Jerusalem in the versicles of the ninth responsory. For just in this way our most holy pilgrim pushed on from Italy to Greece, from Greece to Judea, and again from Judea to Greece, from Greece to Italy, and from there to our own land safe at last. Thus our most ingenious musician made first Latin, then Greek, and finally Hebrew versicles, and again Greek and finally Latin versicles. Thereafter he made a most beautiful *historia* for St. Wunebald, and a new one for St. Blase. Moreover, that same bishop loved (*diligebat*) a very important lady named Pia, who is reputed to have incomparably surpassed all women of her day by the distinction of her handicraft (*artificiorum subtilitate*). She adorned our church with many a marvelous ornament, not only by working and setting a model herself, but also by teaching many others many varieties of artistry. At last, giving herself over wholly to the Lord, she built nearby a convent for nuns, called Bergen, which she enriched with an endowment befitting royalty (for she was extremely rich) and adorned with every kind of art object before she turned it over to the special protection of the Church of Rome. John, the Apostolic Vicar, confirmed this deed with his privilege, which is in our possession today; and proclaimed a most terrible anathema against everyone doing any injustice to that convent.[29]

---

[29] The bishops' list of Gundechar II, bp. of Eichstätt, 1057–1075 (Mon. Germ. Hist., *Scriptores,* VII, p. 244): "Musicus inde locum Regenoldus rexit eundem. Sedit a. 24. 989° anno 2 Non. Apr. ob." Gundechar himself dedicated a new church in Eichstätt to St. Nicholas (*ibid.,* p. 247). *Haserensis* (p. 255) calls Reginold *crisostomus noster.* Gundechar's Pontifical, now in the episcopal archives at Eichstätt, has been thoroughly studied. The basic description is in Pertz' *Archiv* IX (1847), pp. 561–574; for bibliography, see Michel Andrieu, *Les ordines Romani du haut moyen âge,* I (Louvain, 1931), pp. 117–18. Nicholas is included among the bishop-saints in the *ordo ad dedicandum aecclesiam* (p. 124).

Authorship of the Liturgy

Meisen cited[30] no fewer than four later chroniclers of Upper Germany who recorded that *Reginoldus musicus* created a *historiam* of Nicholas, and he quoted Staindel (*saec.* xv) to the effect that *das Nikolausoffizium Reginolds* was spread throughout the German Church. Yet Meisen held to his belief in a Norman composer, and joined Paul Lehmann in denying that such a cursus of Reginold's now existed, if indeed it ever had.[31] To be sure, these four chronicles (*Auctarium Garstense; Annales sancti Rudberti Salisburgenses; Annales sancti Trudperti; Annales CLM 24571*) may well have copied this particular from *Haserensis*. But the point is not the quality of the information; it is the evidence of exceptional interest throughout Upper Germany in an office of Nicholas, and the implicit testimony that it was so exceptional in composition that, in an age which cultivated anonymity, readers were interested in the personality of the composer.

Meisen was not himself in the dark about the technical meaning of the word *historia,* but it seems to have made no impression on him, for he passed over it as of slight moment. Before him, Karl Young had sufficiently documented and defined the relevant meaning: "*Historia* is the name given to the whole series of antiphons and responsories for the Canonical Office, or *cursus,* of a single day, especially when any, or all, of these musical pieces are given in metrical form or adorned with rhyme. *Historia,* in other words, indicates the musical skeleton of the *cursus,* to the exclusion of the psalms and *lectiones,* the musical pieces being more or less versified ... From the tenth century onward, *historiae* of this sort were composed in very large numbers, especially for honoring particular saints or patrons."[32] After documentation, he transcribed the Nicholas liturgy from St.-

---

[30] Pp. 77–79.

[31] Strangely enough, through a series of references at second hand, an author in *Archiv für Liturgiewissenschaft* II (1952), p. 204, cites Meisen as source for belief that Reginold *did* create a cursus for Nicholas Day.

[32] *Manly,* pp. 257–258; cf. his *Drama of the Medieval Church,* II (1933), p. 310, n. 2; Auda, pp. 52, 68–69.

Maur-des-Fossés as an instance.[33] The Nero text differs from this definition only in having in addition the proper lections and an outline of the mass with texts of those propers. Young's evidence settles the question whether Reginold composed a *vita* or an office. The absence of any evidence that a second liturgy existed in the period under discussion is ample warrant for asserting that Reginold composed the extant text.[34]

This office, the words and melodies of which were composed about 960, unquestionably had precedents enough for its verbal structure, as is clear from the Compiègne Antiphonary; but its melodies may have been novel. Whether the introduction of any new melodies, however conventional, would have been impressive in itself, or whether Reginold's compositions were exceptionally impressive musically, we do not know. But we can be sure that they attracted wide attention and that their popularity created a wave of imitation and a further expansion of the ritual of the year. The *Haserensis* states that as a youth Reginold had traveled to Greece. He was, it would appear, a layman at the time. It is possible that by Greece was meant only the Byzantine provinces of Italy with which his emperor was then preoccupied. In that Graecized region special offices for saintly patrons, for which composers like Theodore the Studite were exercising their talents, had reached maturity. Reginold certainly held to the western arrangement of anthems and responses (it may be doubted that he comprehended the Greek language, despite the statements of the chroniclers), but he may

---

[33] This technical sense arises from, *e.g.*, the usage of Amalarius of Metz; after giving the sequence of antiphons and responses, he remarks: "Hucusque historia praesentis festivitatis declarata est." (ed. Hanssens, *op. cit.*, III, p. 91, line 22; cf. p. 93, lines 33, 40). Sichard's *Mitrale* (*ca.* 1200) ix, 2 (*Pat. Lat.*, CCXIII, 406–407), sketches the Nicholas office and adds: "Ex hac ergo legenda hodierna compaginatur historia." The sketch does not depart from the legends of the Nero text. Throughout his work, Sichard applies the term *historia* only to certain offices: Holy Trinity (col. 385), Andrew (406), Lucia (407), Stephen (408), John (408), Innocents (409), Cathedra S. Petri (411), Peter and Paul (417), Stephen (419), Lawrence (419), Decollatio Joannis Baptistae (421), Conceptio B.V.M. (421), Michael (422), Martin (431), Caecilia (431). The list seems to suggest the additions to the *usus pristinus*.

[34] *Revue Bénédictine*, LI (1939), pp. 62–63.

Authorship of the Liturgy

have absorbed some degree of Greek melody.[35] I am not competent to discuss problems of music; for such discussion I refer the reader to Professor Reaney's essay (Appendix B). What I say hereafter will be limited to the verbal texts; therein I add data to demonstrate further that Reginold was their author.[36]

---

[35] Jacques Handschin gives some notion of the complexity of the problem as well as some evidence of the diffusion of Byzantine liturgical patterns in the west, "Sur quelques tropaires grecs traduits en latin," *Annales musicologiques,* II (1954), pp. 27–49.

[36] In the flush of the counterreformation the Church of Eichstätt eliminated all propers of the confessors from the breviary; but so strong was the protest (*tam clerum quam populum gravissime scandalizaret*) that the names of saints of local veneration were restored. However, though St. Nicholas appears in the calendar, no commemoration is recorded beyond that of the Clementine Breviary: "VI Decembris. In festo S. Nicolai Episcopi et Confessoris. duplex. Omnia ut in Breviario." *Proprium Festorum Diocesis Eystettensis . . . auctoritate Ioannis Christophori Episcopi Eystettensis,* Ingolstadt (1619), p. 4.

CHAPTER VII

Otloh's *Vita S. Nicolai*

OTLOH (CA. 1010–1070) was educated first at Tegernsee and then (1024) at Hersfeld. Based at St. Emmeram in Regensburg but sometimes deserting it for posts in other German abbeys, he composed and edited a wide variety of spiritual, didactic, and edifying works,[1] among them either one or two Lives of St. Nicholas. Was it one, or two? He stated in his *De temptationibus,* written late in life, that he had composed a Life at the request of the brothers of St. Emmeram. Dümmler identified a Life of Nicholas extant in Munich MS, *CLM 14419* (*saec.* xii) as Otloh's work.[2] Wattenbach later transcribed the prologue and the final chapter of it,[3] and the Bollandists compared[4] the manuscript text with the texts of certain Austrian and Bavarian legendaries by transcribing selected initia. However, its prologue says nothing about the brothers; it is dedicated to Wicrad, abbot of Fulda: "... primo dehinc, O venerande simul et karissime abbas Wicrade, vestre libellum presentem dignitati recensendum offero ... cuius etiam peticione scripsi." Otloh lived for four years from 1062 at Fulda.[5] He explained to Wicrad that the work was *alienum,* inasmuch as, except for the prologue and one chapter, he had merely assembled a Life from two existing ones. He did not wish to sign his name. He then described his two sources: one was in common circulation, to be found in many places; the other had been transmitted by someone unknown, who said that he had acquired it far away on the Greek borders. Otloh then stated that in composing this Life he had added nothing of his own; in-

---

[1] E. Dümmler, Über den Mönch Otloh," *Sitzungsberichte* (Berlin), 1895, 48, pp. 1071–1086; Manitius, II, 83–103.
[2] See Wattenbach's *Deutschlands Geschichtsquellen,* 4 Aufl., II, p. 55.
[3] *Neues Archiv d. Gessellschaft f. ä. d. Geschichte,* X, pp. 408–409.
[4] *Anal. Boll.,* XVII (1898), pp. 204–210, and repr. in *Cat. Cod. Hagiogr. Namur.* (Boll., *Subsidia Hagiogr.,* 25, 1948), pp. 37–45.
[5] See *Pat Lat.,* CXLVI, 53B. 55A; Manitius, II, p. 85.

Otloh's Vita S. Nicolai

deed, he had abridged both sources, editing out *rusticitas* and prolixity. Where the two agreed, he followed one, but where they disagreed he selected the facts that seemed *melius*.

The full text of this Life in the Munich manuscript, which I shall hereafter call M, has never been published; I have used microfilm kindly supplied by the Bayerische Staatsbibliothek. The outline below will indicate why publication has not seemed necessary. In the outline I shall refer to a second Life, from Namur MS *15* (*saec.* xiii, St. Hubert, Ardennes),[6] as N, and a third Life, from Paris, B.N. MS *Lat. 5284* (*saec.* xiii, of unstated provenience),[7] as P. There is also an "Old Greek Life," transcribed by Falconius, pp. 1-29, from Vatican MS *Gr. 821*,[8] which I refer to as G. M begins fo. 20^v, immediately following the *Vita S. Alexis*,[9] with the Prologue as transcribed by Wattenbach, and then proceeds:

1. Fo. 21^r: *Incipit Vita Sancti Nycolai*. Nicolaus ex illustri prosapia ortus ... puero inponere curaverunt.

The first half, copied and abridged from John the Deacon (*BHL* 6105; Mombr. 296.35-297.28), treats birth and lactation. The second half, the report of this miracle to his uncle, a bishop Nicholas, parallels G, pp. 1-2.

2. Fo. 21^v: *De Muliere Quaedam*. Crescente autem puerulo ... efficiatur societate sanctorum. [*BHL* 6132]

G, p. 2. P, pp. 503-504 (3), paraphrases with occasional (but unmistakable) verbal duplication. N (147.21-23) summarizes.

3. Fo. 21^v: *De Mansione sancti viri celitus ostensa*. Homo quidam sabbatius ... praeparare dignatus est. [Not listed *BHL*]

G, pp. 3-4. Not in P. N (p. 144, no. 4) paraphrases with verbal duplication.

4. Fo. 22^r: *De Puellis ab incestu ereptis*. Quidam familiaris beati viri ... irreprehensibilem vitam duxit.

The *Three Daughters*. Not in G or P. No verbal agreement with John the Deacon or with N (pp. 143-144, no. 3). The emphasis upon

---
[6] Published *Anal. Boll.*, II (1883), pp. 143-151.
[7] Published in *Cat. Cod. Paris.*, I (1889), pp. 503-511.
[8] Francois Halkin, *Bibliotheca Hagiographica Graeca* (Bollandistae, *Subsidia Hagiographica* VIII^a, 1957) II, p. 139, No. 1347. The manuscript was transcribed in the year 1077, according to Anrich, II, 3. 142 ff., who also edited it.
[9] *BHL*, No. 286; *Acta SS*, Jul. IV, 251-253.

incoestus, however, indicates that John was the immediate or eventual source.

5. Fo. 22^r: *Qualiter sanctus vir electus sit ad episcopatum.* Inter haec vero mirae...pontificalem accepit infulam.

Copied from John (Mombr. 299.26-40) with slight variation. N (p. 144, no. 5) paraphrases without verbal duplication. Not in G or P.

6. Fo. 22^v: *De amirabile eius sanctitate.* Kathedra igitur mirensis...sentiretur levamen.

Copied from John (Mombr. 300.11-28). N (144.42-143.4) summarizes. Not in G or P.

7. Fo. 23^r: *De Nautis a tempestate maris liberatis.* Quadam namque die dum quidam naute...benedicentes deum.

Copied from John (Mombr. 300.28-51). N (145.4-15) paraphrases, but with verbal identity in places. Not in G or P.

8. Fo. 23^r: *De diabolo a cypressi arbore fugato.* Quodam quoque tempore a plamitarum castello...persequitur Nicolas. [*BHL* 6147]

G, pp. 4-5. P, p. 508 (18) is verbally similar. N (147.24-27) summarizes with slight verbal agreement. This legend cannot be related to that of Boniface's Oak of Thor (Willibald, *Vita Bonifatii,* 8), composed *saec.* viii.

9. Fo. 23^v: *De fonte populis restituto.* Turba multa de castello arnivedensi...suffere sancti Nicolai. [*BHL* 6134]

G, pp. 6-8. P, p. 504 (5) is verbally similar. N (147.28-31) summarizes, with agreement in names.

10. Fo. 24^r: *De demone ab homine expulso.* Eodem tempore tres homines...deo gratias agebant et sancto Nicolao. [*BHL* 6136]

G, p. 9. P, p. 505 (7), is verbally similar. N (147.33-36) summarizes, with agreement in names.

11. Fo. 24^r: *De Ceco unctione olei a sancto viro sanato.* Quidam cecus nomine antonius...meruisset videre lumen. [*BHL* 6135]

G, pp. 12-13. P, pp. 504-05 (6), is verbally similar. Not in N.

12. Fo. 24^v: *De quodam homine viscerum doloresa nato.* Post haec alter quidam egrotus...glorificans deum. [*BHL* 6137]

G, p. 13. P, p. 507 (8), is verbally similar. Not in N.

13. Fo. 24^v: *Pro leticia clericorum refectionem facta.* Cum quidam clerici reverendi congregati...miracula operetur. [*BHL* 6138]

G, p. 14. P, pp. 505-506 (9), is verbally similar. N (145.37-41) summarizes with some verbal agreement.

Otloh's Vita S. Nicolai

14. Fo. 25ʳ: *De lapide magni ponderis in edificium collocato*. Cum pergeret beatus NICOLAUS...obediant ei. [*BHL* 6139]

G, p. 15. P, p. 506 (10) is verbally similar. N (148.1–3) summarizes with some verbal agreement.

15. Fo. 25ᵛ: *Qualiter sanctus vir quosdam sterilitate coniugii pro querentes fructum adipisci fecerit*. Vir quidam et uxor...ad propria remearunt. [*BHL* 6140]

G, pp. 15–16. P, p. 506 (11), is verbally similar. N (147.31–32) summarizes without verbal agreement.

16. Fo. 25ᵛ: *De Puella arida oratione sancti viri sanata*. Alio tempore duo...glorificans deum. [Not listed *BHL*]

G, pp. 16–17. Not in P. N (148.8–9) summarizes with some verbal agreement.

17. Fo. 25ᵛ: *De demone agnito qui se in angelum formavit*. Illud etiam de sancto viro...ante faciem eius in illa hora. [*BHL* 6141]

G, pp. 17–18. P, pp. 506–507 (12), is almost verbally identical. N (148.4–7) summarizes with some verbal agreement.

18. Fo. 26ʳ: *De Ministro admone arrepto*. Non multo post intravit diabolus in coquinam...non ausus est illum vexare. [*BHL* 6142]

G, pp. 17–18. P, p. 507 (13), is almost verbally identical. N (148.9–12) summarizes, with some verbal agreement.

19. Fo. 26ᵛ: *De frumento navibus adducto*. Alio quoque tempore revertentes ab alexandria...petissent non tribuissent.

Not in G or P. A careful paraphrase, with no more than accidental duplication of words, of John (Mombr. 300.52–301.18). N (145.16–33) paraphrases the same passage in John with considerable verbal duplication, but does not duplicate M.

20. Fo. 26ᵛ: *De oleo in mari viri iussu proiecto, et arsura in aqua*. Interea venerunt ex longinquo...eius precibus evanissent.

The Diana legend paraphrased from John (Mombr. 301.22–302.7). N (147.2–20) paraphrases, but with verbal duplication. Not in G or P. *Arsura*, whence "arson"; cf. *Acta Sebastiani Martyris*, 12 (*Pat. Lat.* XVII, 1118); Ekkehard, *Casus S. Galli* (Mon. Germ. Hist., *Scriptores* XI, p. 128, in referring to burning of St. Gall).

21. Fo. 27ʳ: *De homine in somnis a sterquilinio liberato*. Cum sederet beatus NICOLAUS in arnivedensi castello...et sanctum NICOLAUM. [*BHL* 6144]

G, pp. 7–8. P, pp. 507–508 (15), with some verbal agreement. N (147.29–31) mentions.

22. Fo. 27ᵛ: *De diabolo qui sanctum virum terruit.* Quadam nocte sancto NICOLAO... facie evanuit. [*BHL* 6145]

G, p. 17. P, p. 508 (16), almost identical. Not in N.

23. Fo. 27ᵛ: *De lxx viris de uno pane faciatis.* Est et aliud miraculum... dederunt et beato Nicolao. [*BHL* 6143]

G, p. 18. P, p. 507 (14), almost identical. N (147.42-44) summarizes.

24. Fo. 28ʳ: *De tempestate maris sedata.* Quodam tempore cupiens ... virtutes faceret. [*BHL* 6148]

G, pp. 10-11. P, pp. 508-509 (19), almost identical. N (148.13-18) summarizes with verbal duplications.

25. Fo. 28ʳ: *Qualiter vir sanctus quosdam de periculo mortis liberaverit.* Dum in frigiae partibus... leticia remisit ad propria. [*BHL* 6106]

Stratilates, copied without change from John (Mombr. 302.8-305.50). Not in G or P. N (145.34-147.1) paraphrases and shortens without verbal duplication.

26. Fo. 32ᵛ: *De obitu sancti NYCOLAI.* Factum est ut iret... tempore ioviani imperatoris. [*BHL* 6154, 6156]

G, pp. 28-29. Not in P, or in Mombritius' version of John. N (148.19-26) paraphrases with marked verbal identity. Falconius' version of John, which adds the Sion series at the end of an authentic but corrupt text, was taken from Vatican MS *Regin. Lat. 5696,* and a Neapolitan manuscript "in Lombard script"; pp. 122-124 (nos. 17-18) closely paraphrase this section, with frequent verbal duplication.

27. Fo. 32ᵛ: *Quanta miracula ex tumbi sancti viri fiant.* Postquam igitur beatissimus... portum maris adriatici. [*BHL* 6160]

Not in G or P. Identical with Falconius' version of John, p. 124 (19). Mombritius' version of John (306.2-12) has similar content. N (148.29-41) paraphrases with slight verbal duplication.

28. Fo. 33ʳ: *De Cedrone et filio eius.* Aliud quoque ingens miraculum... videre antequam moriar. [cf. *BHL* 6167]

Verbally almost identical with Mombritius' addendum to John (307.48-309.50). This legend, with boy named Basilios instead of Adeodatus, appears in pseudo-Methodios, as published by Falconius, pp. 58-65, from Vatican MSS *Gr. 281* and *824.* A close analogue, appearing in the *Menologium die 23 Aprilis* for St. George, may have appeared at the end of *saec.* ix, but Anrich, II, 407 ff., found no manuscript evidence of the Nicholas version before *saec.* xi (cf. Meisen, pp. 253-254). This legend is one of four dramatized in the Fleury Playbook (see below), and was known to Alphanus of Salerno, d. 1085 (see *Analecta Hymnica* XXII, No. 348, St. 17). Since this passage comes between Otloh's Prologue and his personal legend, it appears not to be an addendum, and is therefore as early a text as any recorded, though the addendum to John apparently comes from the same source.

29. Fo. 34ᵛ: *De sancti Nycolai imagine a barbaro inventa.* Dum de affrice partibus Wandalorum...committentes ei se et omnia sua. [*BHL* 6164]

Iconia, another of the legends of the Fleury Playbook. Not in G or P. Duplicates without editorial change both Mombritius' addendum to John (306.33-307.47) and Falconius' edition of John, following the Sion portions (pp. 124-136). Falconius printed (pp. 82-86) the Greek version from Vatican MS, *Gr. 821.* Anrich (I, 342; II, 430) says it arose from Calabria *ca.* 1000. Since items 28 and 29 regularly are linked in the earliest texts, it seems probable that they were added to an exemplar of John's *Vita* in southern Italy, and that Otloh had a copy (cf. Meisen, pp. 261-262). However, there is no suggestion that these were known to Reginold. The invocation by the fraternity of St. Emmeram of St. Nicholas as protector against theft (see next item, No. 30) strongly suggests that this famous *Iconia,* so popular in later centuries, was already well known at Regensburg.

30. Fo. 36ʳ: *De furto per sancti Nycolai invocationem prodito.* Contigit etiam in nostro monasterio...sub neglegentia habebatur.

Otloh's own legend of St. Emmeram, ed. Wattenbach, *op. cit.* However, Wattenbach did not note that above *ecclesiam* a scribe wrote in *civis Emmerammi.* For later appearances of this legend, see Meisen, p. 92, n. 1.

M is followed in the codex by an edited version of Nicephorus' account of the Translation (*BHL* 6179).

These data lead to certain conclusions. As Otloh testified in his Prologue, M is a conflation of two Lives, followed by an original contribution concerning a thief at St. Emmeram. From his description and a glance at the content as outlined, we can identify those two Lives. The first, which Otloh called popular, is that of John the Deacon, with additions evidently made in southern Italy, from which Otloh took the first half of No. 1

and Nos. 4–7, 19–20, 25, 27–29. He paraphrased Nos. 4 (*Three Daughters*), 19 (*Corn Ships*), and 20 (*Diana*); the rest are, as it were, copied with only editorial or later scribal changes. We can understand why Otloh paraphased three legends: in them especially John lost himself in rhetoric. Otloh described the second work as anonymous, but coming from the Greek border. An exact Latin source does not exist, but G, the Old Greek Life, contains all of Otloh's material not found in John, and in somewhat the same order. G also contains a good deal of stereotyped legendary matter which is not represented in M, and is basically not a Life of Nicholas of Myra at all, but the Life of a Lycian monk, Nicholas of Sion, who lived in the sixth century. However, the compiler made it accord superficially with the Life of Nicholas of Myra, leaving many internal contradictions and anachronisms. G does not, however, contain any of the material included in John's Life. Since Otloh speaks of duplication, we may assume that the author of whatever Latin recension he had before him had made changes in G.

Although no Latin version of G is extant, to my knowledge, an examination of the above outline will show that P, the Life in the Paris manuscript, a codex which also contains the Cluniac legend of the introduction of the *historia* as given above, duplicates G, but contains none of Otloh's matter not taken from G. In other words, the present P represents, to an indeterminable extent, the anonymous Life which Otloh used; and it is the only known representation.[10]

We come now to N, a Life extant in Namur MS *15*, copied

---

[10] An "infimus Johannes presbiter et monachus," who contrasted himself with "Johannes subdiaconus sanctae Parthenopensis [Neopolitanae] ecclesiae," translated from Greek a *sermo de obitu sancti Nicolai*, which is described by Hofmeister in *Münchenermuseum für Philologie des M.A. und der Ren.* (hgb. Fr. Wilhelm) IV (1924), pp. 135–138. It is impossible to determine when this John lived, except that the edited manuscript (Vienna, *Lat. 739*, fos. $174'^{b}-178'$, $203-203'^{a}$) and another in the Vallicelli Library, Rome, are both *saec*. xii. This John's remarks, as given by Hofmeister, suggest him as a possible transmitter of the material of G and P. Again, Wazelin II, named prior of St. Laurent, Liège, in 1136, and later named abbot, is recorded to have edited a Life and Miracles of St. Nicholas (see Auda, *La musique,* p. 31). Could he have been involved in the P redaction?

Otloh's Vita S. Nicolai

in Lorraine, almost certainly at the abbey of St. Hubert near Liège, during the thirteenth century. Examination of the outline indicates that N is an abridged and almost wholly reworked version of M. Not only does it contain the same legends in a very similar order—so similar as to preclude the possibility that two authors independently conflated the same two sources—but there are enough verbal identities to assure a direct relationship of the two. Moreover, the last chapter is that of M, the legend of the thief of St. Emmeram. The author of N abridged the G portions of M far more than the John portions. N, unlike M, has no prologue, but immediately before the last chapter is a statement which duplicates M's prologue in content:

Ecce quanta potuimus brevitate diximus ea quae percepimus de miraculis sancti Nicolai, quae per ipsum dignatus est Dominus operari ad laudem et gloriam nominis sui, ut nos quoque beato Nicolao impenderemus aliquid officii religiosa intentione, etsi non possumus pia conversatione. Dignum est enim ac necessarium nobis recolere continua veneratione merita sanctorum in quibus jubemur Dominum laudare, ut ipsi dignentur nobis misereri de sua requie, qui in similitudine carnis nostrae experti sunt quondam quia corpus quod corrumpitur aggravat animam, nisi benedixerit Dominus terram suam.

Primus quidem aut inter primos scripsit de vita sancti Nicolai Methodius patriarcha graeco sermone; quem secutus est Johannes quidam diaconus de monasterio sancti Januarii, unus nimium perplexa locutione, et materiam tam felicis historiae quae celebranda est potius ecclesiastica puritate ac simplicitate, depinxit multum per omnem modum scholastico flore et poetico carmine, ut videatur caliginem pariter intulisse cum tanto miraculorum fulgore, dum studebat, utpote xxv annorum tirunculus, nimium verbosus existere. Cetera vero miraculorum insignia quae non habentur in ipsius Johannis scriptura, reperimus in alterius scriptoris editiuncula. Quae si videantur alicui incredibilia, quasi fuco mendacii decolorata, non imputabitur nostro studio vel operi hujus incredulitatis causa, sed magis primario scriptori per quem ad nos est delata, qui ea amplectimur, colimus et veneramur pro beati Nicolai veneratione dignissima, quibus est haec fixa sententia quod apud Deum omnia sunt possibilia. Ceterum discat omnis religio omnisque sexus et conditio quanta dignus sit reverentia ac celebritate, quem Deus tanto dignum ducit honore ut quicumque speraverit in ejus nomine, non privetur optata consolatione.

The Life has been prepared for contemplation in the Office: *ut nos quoque beato Nicolao impenderemus aliquid officii religiosa intentione....* The author has used two works, John's *vita* and *alterius scriptoris editiuncula.* The writer is a brother, working for brothers. He is scholastically critical and sceptical; John's rhetoric annoys him, and the legends of the second source (equivalent with G) strike him as incredible, if not purple lies. There is even grim humor in urging on his brothers the firm belief that with God all things are possible.

Where and by whom was N written? After the paragraphs quoted, the author proceeds: *Sed ad comprobandum beati Nicolai erga omnes sui veneratores patrocinium, referre volumus in calce hujus opusculi quod contigit nostris temporibus in provincia Noricorum et in monasterio sancti Emmerami.* There follows the legend of the thief, paraphrasing but not at all verbally duplicating Otloh's M. Since in M Otloh testified that the theft took place at St. Emmeram in his days, the *nostris temporibus* of N indicates that the two works are contemporary. *In provincia Noricorum et in monasterio sancti Emmerami* suggests that the work was compiled elsewhere than at St. Emmeram or in Bavaria. But we have noted above (No. 30) that even in M a scribe added an identification to Otloh's text. And the *Translatio S. Dionysii,* composed exclusively for the use of the monks of that abbey, and useless elsewhere, reads: "Sub temporibus modernis Noricis contigit terris...hic idem sub tempore jam contiguo translatus est Norico in Emmerammi beati coenobium satis celebre et famosum."[11] It would be even more natural for N, copied in Lorraine, to contain such a statement, originally or as a scribal gloss. It seems most unlikely that two different monastic scholars would conflate two, and only two, source works in so identical a fashion, and I therefore pre-

---

[11] See *Anal. Boll.* I, pp. 494-95.

sume that N, like M, originated with the pen of Otloh. Probably he composed M at Fulda, where he may have found, for the first time, the anonymous work, and possibly even the later version of John. Later, when he returned to St. Emmeram—possibly without M, about which he professed to be abashed—he acceded to the requests of his fraternity to create a set of lections for the Nicholas Office; but having endured the bombast of John and the mendacity of the anonymous author, he freely abridged and paraphrased, with but slight verbal duplication. N, then, seems to be the *Vita S. Nicolai* which Otloh stated in *De temptationibus* that he had prepared for his brothers at St. Emmeram. As with M, he preferred not to attach his name, probably not alone because of the slight degree of originality but also because of the quality of the content.[12]

Without publishing more than the initia of M, the Bollandists (*op. cit.*) compared it with three breviaries, emanating from one author, by arranging the initia in parallel columns so that the parallel structures are manifest. The three manuscript breviaries are from (1) Heiligenkreuz, *saec.* xii^2, (2) Melk, *saec.* xiii, and (3) Windberg (dioc. Regensburg), *saec.* xii^2.[13] These indicate that the anonymous author of the breviaries, using one or both of Otloh's works as a guide or outline, returned to Otloh's two sources in order to compose his own work; for, first, the initia paraphrase but do not duplicate, and, second, the breviary text contains sections from both John (e.g., 27 = *BHL* 6107 = Mombr. 305.53–306.15 = Falc. p. 126) and G (24–25 = G, p. 19 = P, pp. 509–510 [20]), which are not found in M or N. These data concern the present theme only as they indicate Bavaria as the center of dissemination of a cult of St. Nicholas based on

---

[12] As he grew older, Otloh became increasingly ascetic and puritanical; indeed, he seems to have been reactionary among his brothers at St. Emmeram (see Pietzsch, pp. 122 ff. and refs.). Although he considered St. Nicholas an appropriate subject for such a prelate as the abbot of Fulda, it could have been personally distasteful. In all his own writings he shows true veneration only for Antony and Benedict among the post-apostolic saints. Nevertheless, he included Nicholas among the invoked saints in his vernacular prayer, *Pat. Lat.*, CXLVI, 428B.

[13] *Anal. Boll.*, XVII, pp. 27, 32, 93, 96, 119.

the Old Greek Life of Nicholas (of Sion) as well as on the Life by John the Deacon.

N has embodied in it sections of Reginold's liturgy verbatim. In the text of the liturgy, I have noted the verbal identities for the anthems *O pastor aeterne* (2), *Pontifices almi* (18), and *O Christe pietas* (46), and for the responses *Quadam die tempestate* (15), *Audiens Christi* (17), and *Qui cum audissent* (29). Other instances may have escaped my attention. There are also reminiscences without verbal quotation; for example, the anthem *Sanctus quidem triticum* (19) echoes N (7).[14] This is *aliquid officii religiosa intentione;* N is a lectionary directly commenting on the *historia*.[15] Regensburg, the home of St. Emmeram, is but fifty miles down the Altmühl and Danube from Eichstätt, which, though under the nominal supervision of the archbishop of Mainz,[16] considered itself thoroughly Bavarian.

There is another Bavarian composition which betrays evidence of an active Nicholas cult based upon Reginold's *historia*. It is well known[17] that bishop Heribert of Eichstätt (1021–1042) composed two poems identical in melody and rhythm with the anonymous Nicholas-hymn *Plaudat laetitia lux hodierna*.[18] All the evidences of the hymn which Chevalier could cite originate

---

[14] *Anal. Boll.*, II, p. 145.26–29.

[15] See Pietzsch, pp. 128–130, for examples of composers in the generation following Reginold, contemporary with Godehard, who regarded the composition of *vitae* and *historiae* as single operations. For example, Olbert (cf. Manitius II, pp. 457–459), who went to Chartres to study under Fulbert and then returned to Lorraine to teach, becoming abbot of Gembloux in 1012 and of St. James in 1020 (d. 1048), wrote "vitas aliquorum sanctorum aliquibus in locis liquide et polite ... et de gestis eorum in laude Dei secundum regulam musicae disciplinae, in qua multum valebat, dulcissime cantus modificavit. Inter quae quia rogante Raginero comite vitam S. Veroni confessoris composuit, cantum etiam de eo melificavit, antiphonas quoque super matutinales laudes in transitu S. Waldetrudis." Auda, pp. 135, 136, says that the responses for the office of St. Lambert are literally extracted from the corresponding Lection. I have cited other instances above, Ch. V. The abbey of St. Hubert, where N was transcribed, was often a possession of the bishop of Liège. On the secular education in its external school, esp. at the time of master Thierry (*saec.* xi^1), see Kurth, pp. 269 ff.

[16] However, the Nicholas cult was now well established in the archdiocese of Mainz; for example, archbishop Willigis dedicated a church at Weende bei Göttingen to Nicholas about the year 987 (cf. Meisen, p. 80).

[17] Cf. Manitius, II, p. 557.

[18] Chevalier, *Repert.*, II, p. 321, No. 15000. Text in full edited by Mone, III, pp. 453 ff., No. 1091.

in Upper Germany, as do the manuscripts used by Mone for his edition. A study of the text of the hymn indicates that the whole content was drawn from, or at least is limited to, the content of Reginold's *historia,* which utilized only a fraction of the total number of Nicholas legends. From these facts I surmise that Heribert composed the hymn and intended it to harmonize with the *historia.*[19]

It is not to be wondered at that a liturgy composed by a neophyte, possibly a layman, honoring an almost unknown saint should have become popular in Germany in the second half of the tenth century.[20] Otto I, especially from the year 962, had begun establishing the Holy Empire by reorienting the west. No mere symbol was the marriage in St. Peters on Quasimodo Sunday, 972, of the emperor Otto II to the princess Theophano of Byzantium,[21] a marriage negotiated over a five-year period,[22] and in part arranged by the ambassador Luitprand.[23] The extant Nicholas icon of Burtscheid abbey, imported from Byzantium, arrived there through the efforts of Theophano; she was also

---

[19] Another hymn composed in the eleventh century, far more popular, *Exultet aula coelica laetetur* (Chevalier, *Repert.,* I, p. 347, No. 5087; Mone, III, p. 460, No. 1097) is also limited to Reginold's content, but its provenience cannot easily be determined.

[20] In Leopold Delisle's survey of sacramentaries, "Memoire sur d'anciens sacramentaires," *Mem. de l'Institut National de France,* XXXII (1886), pp. 57-423, overwhelmingly derived from France, the name of Nicholas appears in but 3 of 52 examples of the eleventh century and in none of the 75 instances of the tenth century or earlier. Leroquais, in *Bréviaires,* cites about 350 manuscripts with liturgical notice of Nicholas now in French libraries; of these only nine are of the eleventh century and none before the year 1000.

[21] See F. Dölger, "Wer War Theophano?" *Historisches Jahrbuch,* 1949, pp. 646-658, for background and bibliography. We may infer from *Haserensis* that Reginold traveled east between 962 and 966. As a young noble, he may have been a royal legate.

[22] Fliche et Martin, *Histoire,* VII (1948), pp. 58-59; the effective background is perhaps best depicted by Percy Schramm, *Kaiser, Rom, und Renovatio,* Leipzig, 1929, Ch. iii. The history of the relations of Otto and Byzantium has recently been treated, with special reference to Byzantine sources, by W. Ohnsorge, "Die Anerkennung des Kaisertums Ottos I durch Byzanz," *Byzantinische Zeitschrift,* LIV (1961), pp. 28-52.

[23] See his *Legatio* (ed. Joseph Becker). Luitprand supplies us with evidence that the Nicholas cult had not yet impressed the German court. He described in detail (Ch. lxiii) his day at Leucas, and specified that it was December 6; yet he did not call it Nicholas Day or allude to Nicholas. For the literary interests of the Byzantine migrants who followed in Theophano's wake, see Reto Bezzola, *Les origines et la formation de la littérature courtoise* I (1944), pp. 256-258.

responsible for dedicating the abbey to St. Nicholas.[24] The icon is the same effigy of which Caesarius of Heisterbach relates a miracle.[25] With forces largely drawn from Bavaria, the Ottos regularly campaigned in Byzantine Italy, center of a growing Nicholas cult and the homeland of John's *Vita*. In the interest of preserving their Saxon dynasty and of restoring the empire, the Ottos encouraged Graecizing among their German subjects.[26]

A flourishing cult of St. Nicholas, then, existed in Bavaria in the century between 960 and 1060. It was formed first by Reginold's *historia,* then by an exotic Life derived from the "Greek borders," then by two Lives (M and N) that we may presume were both composed by Otloh of St. Emmeram, and then by the Austrian and Bavarian legendaries, extant from three ecclesiastical centers. The codex P, which contains one version of the legend of the Cluniac introduction of the *historia,* also contains the exotic Life. Mayer has observed, without reference to any of these data, "Der Nikolauskult setzt in dem Alperländern und bayerischen Diözesen in der Hauptsache im 11. Jahrhundert ein und schwillt im 12. stark an."[27] Isembert and Ainard of Rouen, German and probably Franconian, composed additions to and adaptations of Reginold's highly original composition, which had attracted the notice of a variety of chroniclers from Bavaria and Austria.

I have already noted that bishop Willigis of Mainz (d. 1011) dedicated a church of his own diocese to St. Nicholas as early as 987. Willigis extended his already great power, acquired under Otto II after the death of archbishop Bruno of Cologne,

---

[24] Meisen, p. 82. Otloh, *Liber visionum,* xvii (*Pat. Lat.*, CXLVI, 372–373), tells of a nun's vision of Theophano's appearing clad in rags and telling of the torments which she suffers in hell because she imported the love of finery into France and Germany.

[25] *Dialogi* viii, 76.

[26] In addition to Schramm, *op. cit.,* see Meisen, p. 81. Eichstätt had a special image in its founder and patron Willibald, whose Asiatic pilgrimages extended for ten years before he spent another ten years at Monte Cassino, from which he was sent on his German mission in 740. On his way out to Jerusalem, his ship ran ashore in Lycia, where he passed the winter; on his way back, he spent two years at Constantinople (see Louis Bréhier, *Les croisades,* 1928, p. 21).

[27] *Archiv für Liturgiewissenschaft,* VI (1960), p. 469, n. 1.

during the regencies of Theophano and of Adelaide, when he was the most powerful prelate, possibly the most powerful noble, in the empire. While under his influence Adelaide became a devout Cluniac, and abbot Odilo, in warm relation with Willigis and Notger of Liège, composed her *vita*.[28] With some reason Willigis regarded the church from Salzburg to Cambrai as a personal domain. He often traveled to Italy with and in behalf of his emperors. I shall speak later of his efforts to retain Gandersheim.

In these efforts he was supported by another powerful prelate of worldly tastes, Notger, bishop of Liège.[29] Notger was born in Swabia and, according to the Annals of Hildesheim, was prior of St. Gall before his elevation.[30] He ruled the diocese which above all other held the balance of power between France and Germany in the days of struggle between the last Carolingians and the Saxon emperors. Even then the speech of the populace was about equally divided between Walloon and German.[31] The artistic remains from Notger's period are clearly Rhenish, much like Cologne's, with the same slight but observable Greek innovations attributable to Theophano. In the last days of Lothaire of Lorraine (d. 986), Notger was named as a Bavarian sympathizer and plotter. Together with his close friend, the scholar and liturgist Heriger, abbot of Lobbes, he accompanied Theophano to Italy in 989–990.[32] In 996 Notger

---

[28] Liège was one of the first churches to introduce Odilo's Feast of All Souls, est. 998; see Auda, pp. 80–81. It is clear from correspondence that Notger favored Cluniac rule.

[29] Kurth, p. 103.

[30] Manitius, II, p. 220; for Notger and Heriger, pp. 219–228. Kurth discounted that annal and maintained (p. 38) that Notger had never been a monk; but see H. Silvestre in *Revue belge de philologia et d'histoire,* XXXI (1953), pp. 69–73. Certainly, despite the two dozen convents which appertained to him as bishop (see the list in Kurth, p. 123), his behavior was unmonastic. His schools, one cathedral and probably six collegial, were markedly secular (Kurth, Ch. XV).

[31] Kurth, p. 245.

[32] "In tantum enim [Herigerus] praedicto venerabili episcopo Notgero charus et familiaris fuit, ut non solum in domesticis vel ecclesiasticis rebus, sed in palatinis quoque negotiis, quorum tunc temporis praecipuus erat excultor, idem episcopus inter primos cum semper habuerit, nec in Lotharingia solum sed et in Italia, ubi Ottoni III adhuc puero regnum praeparabat, eius obsequiis et consiliis usus fuerit." (*Gesta abbatum Lobiensium continuata,* after Kurth, p. 87.)

rendezvoused at Regensburg for the third journey to Italy which he had undertaken in his monarch's behalf; Willigis, as archchancellor, headed the party. The next year he went again, to make Italy, especially Spoleto, the center of his activities until 1002. Kurth[33] notes his importation of a number of cults to Liège, and believes that the chapel of St. Nicholas, recorded in 1241 as *que in ecclesia nostra sita est ante scholas,* was built by Notger.

The Liègeois schools began their great century under the direction of Notger; their power was in part responsible for the rise of diocesan and decline of monastic education. Anselm of Liège describes[34] how Notger drew oblates from the monasteries to be educated at the cathedral, and assembled "librorum copiam ceteraque arma scholaria." Anselm asserts "ut in capellis tam imperatoris quam episcoporum nil magis appeteretur quam cum litterarum studio morum disciplina." Under Notger and his successor Nithard (d. 1041), Wazo directed the schools until he became bishop. Again to quote Anselm: "Domnus Wazo velut Lucifer inter minores stellas enituit" (see Liturgy, No. 4, above).[35] Wazo was master of the schools when Leofric studied there, and was either master or bishop when Giso and Walter were there.

I believe that Liège, where the only extant copy of Otloh's N was copied, was a center for dissemination of the cult of St. Nicholas to France and Britain. Small wonder that the cult spread rapidly and began to center among scholars, for from about 990 to 1050 Liège supplied the greatest number of masters for the schools of western Europe. Silvestre emphasizes[36] the fundamental and important distinction between secular (canonial) and monastic clerics in this period. Not only by tradition but by methods and aims did they live in different worlds—

---

[33] P. 104; cf. p. 153.

[34] *Gesta Episcopum Leodiensium,* 28 (Mon. Germ. Hist., *Scriptores,* VII, p. 205).

[35] 30 (p. 206); see also 40 (p. 211) and 52 (p. 220). A Liège calendar (Brussels MS *1359*), written very early in the eleventh century, has "Sci. nicholai epi." written in the original scribal hand (f. 26^r).

[36] *Revue belge de philologie et d'histoire,* XXXI (1953), pp. 65 ff.

however intermingled might be their vocations. The autobiographical statements of those clergy who on occasion shifted vocation are very convincing in this respect and deserve gathering together as an indication to historians that they need to differentiate more than is customary between diocesan and abbatial schools and education. Clerks imported from Lorraine before the Conquest doubtless contributed to the worldliness of the English church, which had been reformed by Dunstan.

CHAPTER VIII

The Miracle Plays

WHAT APPEAR TO BE the first seven scripts of medieval secular dramas treat legends of Nicholas. Moreover, the first script of an identified author is the Nicholas-play of Hilarius, disciple of Abelard, and Jean Bodel's *Jeu de Saint Nicolas* is by common consent the best secular drama before the fourteenth century.[1] These facts have aroused modern interest.

I shall not review the course of modern scholarship; a few sentences drawn from Young's *Drama of the Medieval Church* (1933) provide enough groundwork for my discussion:

The kind of play which we are now to consider has virtually no associations with Scriptural tradition, and is so peculiarly medieval in its content that, in dramatic history, it has been given a distinctive name of its own. The miracle play, or *miraculum,* may be described as the dramatization of a legend setting forth the life or martyrdom or miracles of a saint... The number of such legends is very large and the body of plays which they inspired during the late medieval period in the European vernaculars is enormous... During the earlier centuries, however, the number of miracle plays designed for use in the churches appears to have been relatively small. The only saint, in fact, whose legends are treated in Church plays that are extant and complete is Nicholas... Concerning the process through which such legends became drama we have no explicit information. One is, of course, attracted by the apparent possibility that, like the plays of Easter and Christmas Day, the dramatic miracula of St. Nicholas arose directly from those kinds of literary embellishment of the liturgy ordinarily known as tropes... We have no evidence, however. In so far as we can judge from the extant miracle plays, they rest not upon short and summary references to the *vita* such as are

---

[1] Not the least of its claims to attention is that it is the first clear precursor of the Shakespearean art of mood-shifting; see Albert Henry, "Introduction Stylistique au *Jeu de Saint Nicolas,*" Romania, LXXXII (1961), pp. 201–239. Henry quotes (p. 238, n.) Siciliano: "Il est impossible de dire où finit le sacré et où commence le profane, il est impossible de distinguer la farce du drame pieux."

[90]

The Miracle Plays

found in liturgical embellishments, but directly upon the complete forms of the legends themselves.[2]

Starting from these sentences, I shall concentrate upon the earliest texts, which appear in three manuscripts: British Museum MS *Additional 22414,* containing two Nicholas plays (*Three Daughters* and *Three Clerks*); Einsiedeln MS *34,* containing a series of verses identified as *Three Clerks;* and Orleans MS *201,* "The Fleury Play-Book,"[3] containing "six strictly liturgical dramas"[4] and four Nicholas plays (*Three Daughters, Three Clerks, Icon,* and *Getron*).

As a preliminary, I wish to object to a common presumption: that the Fleury playbook contains dramatic scripts composed at Fleury, if not by one author or in one period, at least under the inspiration of a common school such as Fleury is believed to represent. Even Young so presumed when he remarked of the Fleury *Icon,* "It is, indeed, surprising that the play-book which shows such ineptitude in managing the three generi in the dowry play [*Three Daughters*] should show such flexibility in the treatment of the *fures* here."[5] It is, in fact, not even certain that the Fleury playbook was copied at Fleury, let alone that the plays were composed there. Normally, one infers of collections of this sort (the Benedictbeuern manuscript, for example) that some wandering student collected an anthology of favorite pieces where he could find them. Opinions about the date of the Fleury manuscript range widely, but center on the year 1200. This is a late date for initial stages of drama, but a proper date for such an anthology.

On the other hand, critics who have venerated the Fleury playbook have neglected the British Museum manuscript: they have slighted the early date, which is regularly described as of

---

[2] II, pp. 307–310. This is essentially the view expressed by Hardin Craig in *Speculum,* XXXVI (1961), p. 698.

[3] Grace Frank, *The Medieval French Drama,* 1954, pp. 44–51.

[4] Albrecht, p. 1. These dramas are: *Officium Stellae, Ordo Rachelis, Visitatio Sepulchri, Peregrinus, Conversio Pauli,* and *Lazarus.* I shall say something of the last two below.

[5] *Drama* II, p. 350.

the eleventh century. Even if it had been copied late in that century, it would be the earliest evidence we have.⁶ But a hand not later than the twelfth century states on the foreleaf, "Lib sc̄i Godehardi · in Hīld · Will."⁷ A small convent dedicated to Godehard was founded in Hildesheim in the year 1146; one might well presume that those words are a bookmark of the convent. But aside from the date of the scribal hand, which is and probably must remain doubtful, it is almost impossible to believe that that small and unscholastic brotherhood would have acquired and inscribed this book. What is much more likely is that whoever wrote those words knew by tradition or local record that the book had been the personal property of the scholar bishop Godehard (1022-1038) himself. If so, it was copied before 1038. The authorship of the plays would be earlier still.

There is general, but not unanimous, consent that *Three Daughters* is the earlier of the two plays. Because attention has concentrated on the Fleury playbook critics have presumed that both plays originated in France. Indeed, even Coffman, who first seriously examined Godehard's connection with them, concluded by repeating the common opinion, that the plays "are essentially the product of French innovations."⁸ But he could offer no evidence to support his assertion.

The strophaic form of composition of the two plays is most important evidence, but since interpretation is complicated by technicalities which cannot easily be reduced to simple conclusions, I have relegated my treatment to Appendix A. At this point I shall merely say that although the strophaic form of the Hildesheim plays yields no certain evidence about proveni-

---

⁶ I have not examined the manuscript, but competent paleographers have. Some useful information is given by Coffman, *Manly*, p. 274, n. 1.

⁷ Manitius, II, 314. On the *monasterium S. Godehardi* in Hildesheim, see *Chronicon Hildesheimense*, 20 (Mon. Germ. Hist., *Scriptores*, VII, p. 855).

⁸ *Manly*, p. 275, n. The prevalent view that the Germany of *saec.* ix–xii owed its culture to France is matched by the views of the political historians; see Barraclough's bitter remarks about Renaud's *Les origines de l'influence française en Allemagne* (1913) in his *Medieval Germany, 911–1250*, 1948, pp. 4–5; cf. pp. 60–62.

The Miracle Plays

ence, the weight of such evidence as can be adduced points to Upper Germany, not France,[9] and to a scholastic hymnographical rather than a liturgical tradition. Von den Steinen has aptly described[10] the peculiar tradition of hymnography: its admission into the Office as a work of art—that is, a product of discipline—regarded as a purely human creation. It is admitted for decor, *glorificatio per laudes*. Hilary and Ambrose exemplified this human composition in non-Hebraic, classical meters. There was no need, as in the *historia* of Reginold, to plead divine inspiration for hymns. They were man's humble offerings. The Nicholas plays were modeled upon the proper hymns to the saints, and the Hildesheim strophe could have been invented in a Bavarian classroom as a properly humble rhythmic counterpart of the more exalted sapphics.

The tetrasyllabic coda of each strophe marks a change of speakers, being identical for successive strophes of each speech, but shifting with each speaker. In all but one (Str. 7), the coda lies outside the syntax of the strophe. These codas are evidence that dialogue, though not necessarily dramatic representation, was consciously composed.

The inscription, *Lib. sci. Godehardi in Hild.*, indicates that Hildesheim tradition attributed ownership, if not creation, of the codex to bishop Godehard. George Coffman pointed out Godehard's vital connection with Nicholas and *Three Daughters*.[11] Briefly, knowledge of Godehard rests largely upon two Lives, both written by his disciple Wolferius, who had studied together with Otloh under Godehard at Hersfeld. Wolferius had migrated to Hersfeld from Hildesheim to study under

---

[9] The earliest French decasyllabic verses, *St. Alexis*, are, following Gaston Paris, generally accepted as the composition of an anonymous canon of Rouen. That canon would almost certainly have been an associate of Isembert and Ainard. The Alexis cult has not yet been systematically traced, but it is known to have arisen in the west after 977 around the church of St. Boniface in Rome (see C. Storey, *La vie de saint Alexis*, Oxford, 1946) with the composition of a Latin Life. Is it a coincidence that Otloh's M in the Munich manuscript follows this Latin *Vita S. Alexis*? The earliest manuscript (*saec.* xii), now at Hildesheim, was written in England by an Anglo-Norman.

[10] *Notker der Dichter*, Darstellungsband, 1948, pp. 82–83.

[11] *Manly*, pp. 269–275.

Godehard, and he returned to Hildesheim when his master was appointed bishop there.[12]

In his *Book of Visions,* Otloh tells of Wolferius:[13]

When, as a boy, I had been sent to the monastery of Hersfeld to learn writing, it came about that I learned of a mighty vision concerning the abbey of Hildesheim. Two canons had been sent from there to our school for tutelage by the bishop Godehard of blessed memory. One of them, named Boto, was younger than I, and the other, Wolfharius, was older. Often we would sit down together to discuss spiritual or worldly matters, and both of them would talk about their homeland. Wolfarius told me about his monastery, saying:

Some years ago it was the custom in our monastery for every one of our clergy to dress in only the most precious vestments, as much for the regular services as for feast days. They had all their seats and hangings in equally rich decor. And the richer each was, the finer he had his furniture. When these fashions had been in vogue for a long time, with no respect for the Heavenly Judge, an angel of the Lord appeared to a neighborhood clerk in a vision, saying: "Hail! And say to the bishop of this city that he should check his own and his clerks' immoderate and irregular ostentation, or else divine vengeance may be visited upon them." Awakening, the clerk disregarded the mandates, rejecting the vision as delusions of sleep. But the angel of the Lord appeared in the same way again to the clerk, and said: "Why did you scorn my advice? Have a care that you do not do so again. For I tell you for certain that if you do not do better, you will not escape unpunished." But the clerk, though to be sure he was considerably shaken at the thought of the vision, nevertheless did nothing about it, as before. Then the third time when the angel came, not as previously warning the clerk in his sleep, but unmistakeably rousing him, the angel said: "How dare you disregard my advice so consistently? Did I not tell you that if you disregarded me any more, you would suffer some vengeance?" The clerk in reply said to him: "I did not act, my lord, in contempt, but because I knew how much the indignation of my bishop, my superior, would be roused by such action, so that, unless I could

---

[12] For the biography of Wolferius, see Manitius, II, pp. 313–318. The *Vitae Godehardi* are in Mon. Germ. Hist., *Scriptores*, XI, pp. 167–218. I have simplified the rather involved relations of these men. Both Wolferius and Otloh also studied at Altaich, though apparently not at the same time. Though Hersfeld was far away, it was essentially Bavarian in personnel and scholastic methods.

[13] *Visio quinta* (*Pat. Lat.*, CXLVI, 357).

The Miracle Plays

give him some sign together with such admonitions, I would run the greatest danger." At this the angel said, "If you need a sign from me, take this for a seal!" So saying, he took up a whip and, striking the clerk with it long and hard, he said: "Mark you the sign that you asked for. If you do not take care to believe our words next time, we shall give you a sign that no one can fail to believe. So go now and carry out our orders." Immediately and without a moment's hesitation, the clerk went to the bishop and recounted the angelic command...

The bishop and his clerks, failing to comply, were severely punished, as it were with the whip of Nicholas. Otloh concludes:

These matters the aforesaid clerk related to me at the time when we were fellow scholars. Now I also relate them for the edification of others, especially for the benefit of those who, when they become pastors of the Church, are placed over others for the outward show of religion...

Wolferius, like Otloh, used Reginold's Nicholas-liturgy verbatim when he composed his *Vita Godehardi*. Coffman[14] quoted Wolferius: "Beatus igitur Godehardus pontificatus infulis decoratus, Nonis Decembris Hildinesheim advenit, omnesque in suo adventu vere gratulantes invenit." He commented upon the significance of Godehard's induction into his see on December 5, Nicholas-vespers. But he did not, of course, note that Wolferius was underlining the significance by quoting Reginold's anthem (No. 41, p. 37 above). There are other identities.

Born about the year 960, just when Reginold was composing the liturgy, Godehard became prior of Altaich, and then, with the emperor Henry II as sponsor, became abbot and reformer of that abbey and those of Hersfeld and Tegernsee. An ardent student, scribe, builder, and collector of artifacts, he assembled a large library at Altaich, *mirae pulchraeque quantitatis sed maioris per anni circulum cantandi legendique utilitatis*. When he transferred to Hildesheim in 1022, he continued his masterful habits: "Iuvenes quoque et pueros quos inibi bonae indolis et

---

[14] *Manly*, p. 273, n. 2.

sapidos invenit, per diversa scholarum studia circumquaque dispertivit; quorum certe postea servimine variam ac multiplicem suae ecclesiae utilitatem in lectione scriptura et pictura ac plurali honestiori clericalis officii disciplina conquisivit." Finally:

> It was wonderful how patient and kind he could be to delinquents and trouble-makers—so much so that whenever any of that sort ran to him for confession and penance, he immediately extended clemency to those wrong-doers and watched over them to see that they were freed from temptations of that sort thereafter. He foresaw every future contingency, in the pattern and model of the holy bishop Nicholas, his patron, who with his almsgold removed the maidens' incest (*virginum incestus*), the poverty of their father, and the foul reputation of the whole household; and with his pious clemency he relieved the sufferings of whatever poor might come in contact with him for whatever reason. In that model, I say, our prelate labored to console the needy ever and everywhere.[15]

Wolferius' *auro virginum incestus et patris earum inopiam et totius familiae detestabilem ademit infamiam* is a verbatim repetition of anthem 7 in Reginold's *historia* above. *Incoestus*[16] was not an invention of Reginold, but went back to John the Deacon. Though we might possibly attribute the analogy of *Three Daughters* to Wolferius' invention, we must agree that Godehard and his school, at Hildesheim and previously at Hersfeld, where Otloh studied with him, were devoted to Reginold's liturgy, which would be inscribed in the [*libri*] *mirae pulchraeque quantitatis sed maioris per anni circulum cantandi legendique utilitatis*.

We do not know in any detail the scholastic conditions at Hersfeld, or at Altaich and other Bavarian schools; evidence is not available. But we can compare St. Gall. By the fortunate preservation of much of that rich library, we know how much

---

[15] Mon. Germ. Hist., *Scriptores* XI, pp. 207–208, as in *Manly*, p. 272. The intensity of this Nicholas cult in Bavaria is indicated by Otloh's story of the three-day continuous masses at the time of the St. Emmeram theft.

[16] The solecism led Young to insert an exclamation mark in his text.

The Miracle Plays

modern literature owes to the inventions of its German masters. Among the manuscripts preserved there, we find evidence of expansion of the liturgy by tropes, sequences, and propers in the tenth century—in the school exemplified by Notker Balbulus. Literary invention was rife at a time when provinces to the west were barely surviving the Norman impact. That Upper German school gave us such firsts of medieval literature as the sequence-proses, the formularies, the chivalric epic. These were all invented essentially for the needs of the choir-school, not the choir in divine service, though the two were hardly separable in such a brotherhood. Notker created even his sequences primarily to ease the mnemonic burden of his schoolboys. The formularies, which started *ars dictaminis* on its medieval way, were school texts. From the same scholastic environment arose "the first chivalric epic." Whatever may be the disputes about *Waltharius,* whoever reads it "is amazed at the work of such a youthful poet. The testimony of the last four lines is explicit:

> haec quicumque legis, stridenti ignosce cicidae
> raucellam, nec adhuc vocem perpende, sed aevum,
> utpote quae nidis nondum petit alta relictis.
> haec est Waltharii poesis. vos salvet Iesus."[17]

It has long been clear that the German masters, especially the monastic masters of the external classes, encouraged precocious students to compose something like our prize compositions, modeled on the scholastic *auctores,* but normally (*Waltharius* is an exception) on Christian, and therefore usually hagiographical, subjects. Walafrid's *Visio Wettini* is an early, but outstanding, example. Our first chivalric epic was a product of a medieval classroom which, though located at a monastery, was almost certainly an external classroom, where "canons" studied.[18] The

---

[17] F. J. E. Raby, *Secular Latin Poetry,* II (1934), p. 263.

[18] Wilhelm Meyer stated in ecstatic terms what is here expressed (see *Gesammelte Abhandlungen,* I (1905), pp. 39-40 and esp. pp. 46-47); but he limited his consideration to the effect upon later literature of the sequences.

Ruodlieb, composed at Tegernsee and at one time attributed to Froumond, student with Otloh there,[19] is an early *Parzival.*

What was true of sequences, rhetorical prose, and epic composition was also true of hymnography. It is clear from the words of Notker Balbulus that he had composed hymns before he composed his sequences, which he began about the age of twenty—the time of entry into the subdiaconate.[20] The leading teachers of Bavaria derived their training from Swabia—St. Gall and Reichenau. Ermanrich of Ellwagen is characteristic. The enterprise of Ratpert, Tuotilo, and Notker was exported to the east and flourished there.[21] In short, the most important literary innovations of the ninth, tenth, and early eleventh centuries—the ones which have left the most distinguished mark upon modern literature—came from Upper Germany.

The classroom, the home of the Sapphic hymns, is likely to have been the home of dramatic scripts as well. Though Wolferius' *Vita Godehardi* yields a verbatim quotation from the *historia,* the *Hildesheim* drama of *Three Daughters* has no such verbal echo of the *historia,* unless we count *Siste gradum,*[22] which seems hardly a purposeful repetition. The need for interrelating the lections from hagiography with the chants of the choir is manifested in the *vitae* composed by both Otloh and Wolferius, who studied together at Hersfeld. I have noted above the appearance of this convention is nearly all early *historia.* Hymnography was also a part of both schoolroom and choir. But if the plays had been an intimate part of the *cursus,* as the

---

[19] Pirmin Lindner, *Die Äbte und Mönche der Benediktiner Abtei,* Tegernsee, 1897, pp. 30–32.

[20] Cf. von den Steinen, *op. cit.,* pp. 521, 492.

[21] There was also a flow in the opposite direction. The Nicholas sequence, *Perpes laus et honor* (Chevalier, *Repert.,* II, p. 310, No. 14846; Mone, III, p. 450, No. 1088), extant only in St. Gall MS 380 (*saec.* xi), with neumes, has often been ascribed to Notker, though von den Steinen rejects it; at all events it was almost certainly composed at St. Gall before the eleventh century. It is derived from Reginold's *historia,* as is indicated especially by *sidus claruit mundo* (5), a common figure in Byzantine works on Nicholas which does not appear in John's *vita* or elsewhere than in Reginold's work before the end of the eleventh century. Cf. Nos. 4 and 38 above. *Hic nefas vetuit, auro Puellas eximens stupro* (4), seems also to be derived from 6 above.

[22] Strophe 15 = John (ed. Mombritius), p. 299, line 13.

The Miracle Plays

lections were, presumably they, too, would contain such repetitions, as they do not.

This absence of liturgical connection suggests that the dialogues were prepared for didactic purposes rather than for edification. They are at home in the school, not the sanctuary.

To make such a statement is to recall from almost total neglect by the historians of drama the name of Rosvitha. Rosvitha's home in Saxony is far from Bavaria; but the Saxon Henry II, educated at Hildesheim, had been duke of Bavaria even before he became king. His special concern for the preëminent Saxon see which was also his alma mater was no doubt a forceful reason for his pressure upon Godehard to accept the onerous post at Hildesheim at a time when Godehard was already longing for retirement; he was well acquainted with Godehard's educational work in the south. He would expect Godehard to transfer his pattern of Bavarian spirituality to Hildesheim. We learn from Wolferius some details of how Godehard did so. No doubt Wolferius was only one of several disciples to move with him and to help him to put his educational pattern into effect at Hildesheim.

When Godehard reached the north country, he was immediately involved in the celebrated quarrel over possession of the convent of Gandersheim, which the archbishops at Mainz, Willigis and Aribo, had long been trying to wrest away. Henry II decided against the powerful Aribo soon after Godehard arrived, and in his favor.[23] Gandersheim, which was the school for noble Saxon women, as Hildesheim was for men, lay but a short distance from the bishop's see.

Gandersheim was the home of Rosvitha, the scholastic poetess, who not only celebrated the Ottos in epic verse and composed *vitae,* but created six "dramas" in imitation of Terence which historians have considered unique—unprecedented and unimitated—in medieval literature. Many of these critics contend that Rosvitha had no conception of staged representation; Zeydel

---
[23] *Cambridge Medieval History,* III (1924), pp. 251, 255.

found their number about equally divided on the question.[24] If she did not, the works are scholastic dialogues, in the manner of many, if not most, of the textbooks of the time, on the ample precedents of Augustine's early texts, Martianus Capella, Boethius, and the catechisms, which were followed by Alcuin's writings and the *Caroline Books*. More pertinent are the Carolingian imitations of the eclogues, which comprise a spate of versified *disputationes* and *altercationes,* among those of special relevance being the ninth-century *altercatio* between Terence and Delusor,[25] in which the dialogue suggests dramatic action more obviously than most.[26]

Rosvitha explained her purpose and method:

There are many Catholics, and we cannot entirely acquit ourselves of the charge, who, attracted by the polished elegance of the style of pagan writers, prefer their works to the Holy Scriptures. There are others who, although they are deeply attached to the sacred writings and have no liking for most pagan productions, make an exception in favor of the works of Terence, and, fascinated by the charm of the manner, risk being corrupted by the wickedness of the matter. Wherefore I, the *clamor validus* [= Germ. "Rosvitha"] of Gandersheim, have not hesitated to imitate in my writings a poet whose works are so widely read, my object being to glorify, within the limits of my poor talent, the laudable chastity of Christian virgins in that selfsame form of composition which has been used to describe the shameless acts of licentious women...I have no doubt that many will say that my poor work is much inferior to that of the author whom I have taken as my model, that it is on a much humbler scale, and indeed altogether different...I strive only, although my power is not equal to my desire, to use what talent I have for the glory of Him who gave it to me. Nor is my self-love so great that I would, to avoid criticism, abstain from proclaiming wherever possible the virtues of Christ working in His saints. If this pious devotion gives

---

[24] Edwin H. Zeydel, "Were Hrotsvitha's Dramas Performed During Her Lifetime?" *Speculum,* XX, (1945), pp. 443–456. His article supplies an extensive bibliography on Rosvitha.

[25] The extant fragment ed. P. von Winterfeld, *Hrotsvithae Opera,* 1902, pp. xx–xxii; E. K. Chambers, *Medieval Stage,* II (1903), pp. 426–428; P. S. Allen and H. M. Jones, *Romanesque Lyric,* 1928, pp. 354–355 (English translation, pp. 245–246).

[26] H. Walther, *Das Streitgedicht,* Munich, 1920, pp. 88 ff., traces the development of the tradition; for *Terence,* which Walther calls mimetic, see p. 89.

The Miracle Plays

satisfaction I shall rejoice; if it does not, either on account of my own worthlessness or of the faults of my unpolished style, I shall still be glad that I made the effort. In the humbler works of my salad days I gathered up my poor researches in heroic couplets, but here I have sifted them into a series of dramatic scenes[27] and avoided through omission the pernicious voluptuousness of pagan writers.

There is nothing in this statement that supports the critical inference of half of the recent critics that Rosvitha's compositions are not dramatic scripts.[28] First published by Conrad Celtes,[29] the plays now exist in a Munich manuscript from St. Emmeram (*CLM 14485*), written toward the end of the tenth century, probably copied directly from the exemplar at Gandersheim.[30] Godehard, the indefatigible collector, could hardly have failed to know Rosvitha's dramas before ever he went north to Gandersheim. I imagine that the dramatic activity represented by the *Three Daughters* flowered in Bavaria before he moved; but the point is not important.

Rosvitha's texts are composed in rhymed prose, without stage directions but with definite scenes and with the speakers indicated. All critics remark about the dramatic quality of the prose. As the author says, the plays are primarily concerned with the theme of Christian chastity in adversity. They are based on fables of the fourth century—some taken directly from the *Vitae Patrum*.[31] This period from Constantine to Theodosius was the time when monasticism sprouted with Antony and flowered with Jerome. It was the presumptive time of Nicholas. Three of the six plays (*Gallicanus, Dulcitius, Sapientia*) involve three sisters-german who struggle under threats of a fate worse than death, as do the three daughters of the Nicholas play.

---

[27] "In hoc drammatica vinctam serie colo." ed. Winterfeld, *op. cit.*, pp. 106–107. I have used the translation of Christopher St. John.

[28] The rubric of the manuscript describes the collection as *dramatica serie contextus*, in line with the last sentence of the text above. Not a few critics have maintained that the texts are Humanist forgeries.

[29] Nürnberg, 1501.

[30] Winterfeld, *op. cit.*, p. iv.

[31] "Sumsi ab antiquis libris sub certis auctorum nominibus conscriptis" (p. 105).

Everything in the form and content of Rosvitha's plays supports her description of her purpose and method. All the plays are clearly scholastic imitations of an accepted classical *auctor:* there is no hint of a liturgical connection or of any relation to the sanctuary. There is no suggestion of music or chant.

It is difficult, indeed impossible, for me to believe that these scripts were never "acted out" at Gandersheim. Imagine a classroom given to studying by dialogue directly and through written texts, to the composition of classical imitations, to rote and mnemonic teaching of members of religious choirs in which antiphons and responses were the allotment of individuals, to the practice of tropes which were already developing (so critical theory goes) into liturgical drama. Now, at the same time, imagine that these speaking parts created by Rosvitha were not allotted to individual members of the class for speaking aloud. I cannot.

Otloh is our authority for the affluence of professional *histriones* in the kingdom of Saxony at the time:

Dictum namque mihi est, ut recolo, quia, cum in Saxonia nuptiae cujusdam praepotentis essent agendae et ad has histriones multi, sicut vulgo solvent, properarent venire, quidam histrio et fama et dignitate caeteris praestantior, nomine Vollare, simul properavit. Sed ne tantae dignitatis vir solus pergere videretur, acquisivit sibi alios eiusdem artis gnaros octo et cum eis quasi militibus stipatus ad nuptias profectus est.[32]

This is Otloh's introduction to a tale about Vollare and the Devil. His acceptance of the affluence indicates that *histriones* were equally plentiful and equally listened to in Upper Germany.

We know that Rosvitha's texts were circulated to the male schools at Regensburg, Altaich, and Hersfeld.[33] In those schools the curriculum and the pedagogic methods did not differ essen-

---

[32] *Liber visionum*, xxiii (*Pat. Lat.*, CXLVI, 385). Adam of Bremen is another witness (F. J. Tschau, *Adam of Bremen's History*, 1959, p. 147).

[33] Not only is the unique manuscript from St. Emmeram, but traces of Rosvitha's plays appear in the Austrian *passionale*, which is linked with Otloh; see Zeydel, p. 447, and refs.

The Miracle Plays

tially from those of Gandersheim. The plays would be used as scholastic models. But there would be a rising objection to the effeminacy of the subjects treated. Given the model and given an active and fresh cult of Nicholas, some Godehard or Wolferius would almost certainly be inspired by Rosvitha's three dramas, each with three sisters in distress, to use the Nicholas legend of the *Three Daughters* to convey an equally didactic message, but with a man as hero. Indeed, even the character of the first daughter, who suggests prostitution as the solution, an invention not found in John's *vita,* may well have been suggested by characters in two other dramas of Rosvitha—Maria and Thais. I conclude that Rosvitha's scholastic compositions eventuated in Europe's "first secular drama," the Hildesheim *Three Daughters.*

Yet we cannot be sure that a truly dramatic script was yet realized in the Hildesheim manuscript of *Three Daughters.* Granted that there are a few indications of speakers[34] and that the codas indicate speaking parts, in the main the script far less suggests "representation," in Young's sense of the word, than do the scripts of Rosvitha. Doubtless the quality of authorship partly determined this difference; after all, there were not many so imaginative or responsive as Rosvitha. The decasyllabics of the Hildesheim *Three Daughters* are mediocre verse in more than mere form.

In making this presentation I am obviously indebted to George Coffman, who realized that Godehard was in some fashion a key figure in the development of the Nicholas plays. Coffman believed the texts to be musical, and therefore extensions of the liturgy: "Thus we have here to do with *musical services,* an essential feature of our Miracle Plays."[35] Although I am confident that Coffman was right, that the Hildesheim plays are hymnographical, his phrase "musical services" is, I think, unfortunate, for it suggests religious services. These

---
[34] Young, *Drama,* II, p. 313.
[35] *New Theory,* p. 56 (italics his); see p. 60: "It is clear to one after careful study of the plays that their verse, in form and lyric quality, suggests the medieval Latin hymn."

scripts were composed for the classroom—to be sure, on the model of hymns, which were regularly being composed there—but their purpose was instruction, not worship. The associations of the decasyllabic are paraliturgical and scholastic. Since any worthy hymns composed in school were undoubtedly sung in the office, and since the same boys spent their days in both class and choir, it may seem that I make a distinction without a difference. But I feel that the place of presentation would have been very meaningful to medieval participants and should be meaningful to us.

Young's instinctive rejection, or at least nonacceptance, of this part of Coffman's theory arose from his incomparable mastery of texts which reveal life in the Middle Ages. He realized that these Nicholas dramas are not an extension or commentary upon the office. If the Nero manuscript represents the *lections* of Reginold's liturgy (as we cannot deduce that it does, for the lections were somewhat arbitrarily altered), then Young would be right in saying that there is no evidence that the dramas were drawn from the lections of the cursus; for rather strangely, *Three Daughters* is the only legend of John the Deacon which is omitted in the Nero text. Since the only theory of the development of liturgical drama acceptable to Young was that drama developed from the lections, he concluded that the Nicholas dramas were not liturgical—a reasonable conclusion. But he took one step too far in suggesting that because they were not liturgical they were not connected with hymnography.

Young was puzzled,[36] as was Dümmler before him, by some unintelligible lettering at the end of the Hildesheim text. But the first groups of letters (*Gror̄ g̊pe*) almost certainly stand for *Graciarum ergo pre-,* the initium of a strophe absent in the Hildesheim *Three Daughters,* but present in the Fleury text.[37] That strophe is a kind of unitarian doxology and fit conclusion. The following words, *hospes gaudeto pacemque salutis habeto.*

---

[36] *Drama,* II, p. 314, n. 1.
[37] *Ibid.,* pp. 318, 319, 320.

The Miracle Plays

$\bar{R}$ *hospitis Vobis letis iā Dī eximiā . . . O filie,* almost as certainly are the introduction of the protagonist of the following dialogue or play, with the "cast" of the first *miraculum* greeting the cast of the second; together they chant or recite *Te Deum,* which in this period as in all others was a paraliturgical as well as liturgical hymn of devotion. The appearance of *Te Deum* here and at the end of many dramatic scripts might seem to indicate a connection with the matutinal office, but there is no evidence whatever that it does. Actually, these words at the end of the Hildesheim *Three Daughters* suggest otherwise. The fact that *Te Deum* was sung at the conclusion of the liturgical dramas[38] may have suggested this scholastic interlude; indeed, we can imagine the three daughters of our script being impersonated by the same three boys who sang the parts of the three Marys in the liturgical drama; but again there is no evidence.

The Fleury manuscript of *Three Daughters*[39] is a repetition of the Hildesheim text, but glamorized. Seventeen strophes are identical; hence there can be no question of the source of the Fleury play. There are additional strophes in the same prosody, some with four, some three, some two, decasyllabics before the codas. But if my interpretation of the unintelligible phrase given above is correct, at least one strophe that was in the original composition has been omitted in the Hildesheim manuscript.

However, as a prologue the Fleury text presents two speeches, one for the father and one for the daughters, written in septenarii, thrice punctuated with a heptasyllabic exclamation (*O rerum inopia!*). These verses seem certainly to be later additions. Even without this slight change, the Fleury text represents more complex drama: it is clearly conscious dramatic art, as Young has explained in detail.[40] As with all the other Fleury

---
[38] "Almost invariably the incipit 'Te Deum' is found at the conclusion of a dramatized version [of the Sepulchre Drama]." (*New Oxford History of Music,* II, 1954, p. 179.)

[39] Text in Young, *Drama,* II, pp. 316–321.

[40] *Ibid.,* pp. 321–323.

texts, including *Three Clerks,* neumes indicate its musical form. But Albrecht remarks:[41]

The musical treatment of the four St. Nicholas plays varies considerably in its effectiveness in reflecting the sentiments of the characters. The [*Three Daughters*] has only two different musical stanzas, so that the last thirty-five stanzas are sung to the same melody. As this melody is used for decasyllabic stanzas with refrain, and the music for each of the four lines is the same for the first six syllables, we have melodic interest at a minimum... The [*Three Clerks*] in its musical construction is almost simpler than the preceding play, having only one musical stanza for the whole action of the play, except for the final prayer of the saint.

This observation accords with the evidence of classroom composition; the hymns, as studied there, were grammatical (i.e., literary) texts. At some time between the composition of the text of the Hildesheim manuscript and the revision existing in the Fleury playbook, some one rather hastily and inartistically added music to *Three Daughters* and *Three Clerks* to make them conform more nearly with the developments of liturgical drama or with the tastes of a different audience. Since the verbal texts had been composed on hymnographical principles, the addition of music was not difficult.

The second Hildesheim text, *Three Clerks,* is composed in the same verse form as *Three Daughters,* but the diction is not so similar as to assure us that one author composed both. The fable of *Three Clerks* is:

Three wandering scholars take lodging in a remote inn. The innkeeper and his wife murder them for their money. Nicholas, as a beggar, asks for lodging and calls for fresh meat to eat. When the host denies that he has any, Nicholas exposes the crime and prays to God to restore the clerks.

Three Daughters is given to the most obvious of scholastic rhetorical figures—*opes patris inopes; mee miserie, michi mesto;*

---
[41] P. 102.

The Miracle Plays

luce feror et nocte anxius; vestra vexat; lugens lugendo; doloribus dolores—as well as to some of better quality. *Three Clerks* seems not so self-conscious, and the sentence order is not so stiff. But especially indicative is the incorporation of the coda into the syntax of the strophe. It therefore appears that these two plays were not composed together, though *Three Clerks* may have been a mature production of the adolescent author of *Three Daughters*.

The text concludes with *O Christi pietas. Angelus. Nicolae, vita fidelibus reddita est a Deo [t]uis precibus*. The presumption seems correct that *O Christi pietas* is the initium for anthem 46, which was normally an anthem for either first or second vespers or lauds. We may surmise that Reginold composed it for vespers. But at Bayeux, for example, it was employed at Mass, at Rouen at the Translation, and at Amiens on St. Nichasius Day, when the Nicholas octave concluded. Bayeux also employed it at the evening processional to the chapel of St. Nicholas. For those who would link these plays to the liturgy by means of the concluding anthems, this last use seems most indicative. If, as we know was certainly true at Eichstätt, there was a Nicholas chapel to which a processional moved on Nicholas Day, it would seem possible that these little plays may have been presented at some point during the processional. The same initium concludes the Fleury *Three Daughters*. The *Angelus,* who evidently speaks the words following, is probably the Angel who testified to Sabbatius in Otloh's *Vita* (3) and the Bavarian Legendaries.[42] The words carry out Otloh's admonition: "Ceterum discat omnis religio omnisque sexus et conditio quanta dignus sit reverentia ac celebritate, quem Deus tanto dignum ducit honore ut quicumque speraverit in Eius nomine, non privetur optata consolatione."[43]

There is a problem of importance regarding *Three Clerks,* that is, the provenience of the fable. Except for this Hildesheim

---
[42] Above, No. 3; cf. *Anal. Boll.,* XVII, p. 206; I, p. 144.
[43] N in *Anal. Boll.,* II, p. 151.

manuscript, it does not appear anywhere until Wace, *ca.* 1150, who gave it full treatment in his Romance *Life of St. Nicholas,* lines 213–226.[44] An eleventh-century hymn from Troyes alludes to it:

> Suscitator clericorum
> Signis admirabilis,
> Fac, a morte peccatorum,
> Surgam reus flebilis.[45]

Now this hymn, inc. *Copiose caritatis,* is plainly inspired by anthem 57.[46] Therefore its author was accustomed to Reginold's liturgy.[47]

According to the most popular form of the legend, the innkeeper stores the decimated three clerks in a pickling tub, from which they rise restored through the intercession of Nicholas.

---

[44] Einar Ronsjö, ed., *La vie de Saint Nicolas par Wace* (Études Romanes de Lund, V, 1942), pp. 121–122; cf. pp. 42–44. For a summary of evidence, see Albrecht, pp. 25–43.

[45] *Anal. Hymn.,* XL, p. 305; Chevalier, *Repert.,* IV, p. 85, No. 36403.

[46] Chevalier, *Repert.,* I, p. 232, No. 3864.

[47] Young, *Drama,* II, p. 328, n. 2, says that there are references to *Three Clerks* in the Prose, *Sospitati,* and in the Response 36 and possibly in the Antiphon 20. Isembert could have referred to it in composing *Sospitati,* but the reference is more than doubtful: *Relevatur a defunctis defunctis in bivio. Defunctus,* though possibly a plural, is singular if verse stress marks a long vowel. A variant appearing in the Aberdeen breviary, *Relevabit . . . defunctum,* seems convincing evidence that *defunctus* is singular. If singular, it obviously cannot refer to *Three Clerks.* There are many quite early legends of Nicholas' raising of the dead; for example, the merchant slain by his host (*Cat. Cod. Brux.,* I, p. 315; cf. Meisen, pp. 286–288), or the murdered partner (*Anal. Boll.,* IV, 202–203). Chances are that this line refers to the pseudo-Johannine legend of the cheated Jew, as found in the addenda to Otloh's N (*Anal. Boll.,* II, pp. 153–156), because in that legend the dishonest Christian is stated to have been killed *in bivio,* and then to have been resurrected. This legend is contained in the Austrian-Bavarian legendary (*Anal. Boll.,* XVII, p. 209, No. 33), but not in Otloh's M. *Sospitati* also refers to two other legends, *The Lost Chalice* (see Meisen, pp. 276–280) and *The Icon* (pp. 261–269), which are contained in the same legendary, but not in Otloh's M or N. In E (*Ordinale Exon.,* III, p. 183), *Post primum in capitulo. lectio,* appears a legend given by Wace (lines 1097–1156) of a merchant slain by an innkeeper and restored by Nicholas, for which Ronsjö, *op. cit.,* pp. 40–41, gives a Latin analogue from Paris, B.N. MS *Lat.* 5290 (*saec.* xii), and names six other manuscripts of *saec.* xii. Meisen, who treated the legend, pp. 286–287, knew of nothing dated earlier than Wace.

How Young misinterpreted Nos. 20 and 36 will be made clear below. In this monograph I shall forego treatment of the theme of the *corpus diaboli,* which results in the connection of these murder stories with Nicholas. Suffice it at this time to say that apparently John the Deacon inspired them by his rhetorical proem, ed. Mombritius, p. 297, lines 5–14.

The Miracle Plays

But this play says nothing about a pickling tub;[48] the three clerks (*clerici, litterarum studii*) are slain purely for their money by the innkeeper and his wife together, and are hidden *in manticis*. However, Nicholas' request for fresh meat does lay the groundwork for later embroidery of the tale.[49] Given this cue, an author could certainly develop the theme after the great famine of 1030–1033. Raoul Glaber[50] describes it in long and fearful detail:

Dare we believe it? Those maddened by starvation revived examples of that atrocity so rare in history, and men devoured the flesh of men. The traveller, waylaid on the road, fell beneath the blows of his aggressors; the members were torn away, grilled on the fire, and devoured. Some, fleeing from their own land to escape the famine, accepted hospitality on the roads, and their hosts cut their throats at night to provide nourishment for themselves. Some others held out an egg or an apple to children to entice them into by-paths, and then sacrificed them to their hunger...

This fable of the *Three Clerks* has attracted incalculable scholarly attention as evidence of Nicholas' patronage of scholars and children, the effects of which are still evident. Indeed, both Wace and the author of the Legendary which is found in the same Brussels manuscript that contains the tale of the Bari widow state unequivocally that the tale resulted in the patronage, rather than the other way around. Into the midst of this ocean of discussion we are now in a position to inject two facts.

The first is that Godehard, definitely identified with Reginold's liturgy and with the Hildesheim plays, and stated to be under Nicholas' patronage, was an exemplary scholar of his day and the master of identifiable authors whose own devotion to Nicholas is clear. I cannot doubt that Nicholas' patronage of the master Godehard, specifically attested by Wolferius, was extended to his innumerable and important disciples. His

---

[48] The earliest icons, the Tournai fonts at Winchester and Zedelghem, show the three clerks rising from a prone position; see, e.g., Albrecht, p. 41, and the *Journal of the British Archeological Association*, XLII (1886), pp. 26–34 (on the font at Brighton).

[49] Young, *Drama*, II, pp. 490–491.

[50] *Historiae* II, ix, 17; IV, iv, 10–13.

schools were the most famous in Europe at the moment, save for those at Liège, dominated by Notger and Heriger. But the schools of Liège, too, were demonstrably devoted to Nicholas at the beginning of the eleventh century. For these cults, Reginold's liturgy was clearly responsible.

The second is that the seed of patronage of boys is to be found in the liturgy. The Angel's closing words, *Nicholae, vita fidelibus reddita est a Deo tuis precibus,* are plainly based on Response 36, which in its Verse states the seminal idea of *Three Clerks.* This response was one of Reginold's more original compositions—that is, less directly derived from John the Deacon than most of his compositions. Yet the root is apparent. It is an extension of Response 17 and Anthem 20. John the Deacon had, in his narration of the rescue of the three citizens of Myra, the subplot of *Stratilates,* employed the adverb *innocenter*[51] and followed it with *innocentium cruorum*[52] and *innocentem et iustum.*[53] John's story dealt with mature men; he used the words *cives, viri,* and *iuvenes* interchangeably. But to a transalpine group, *innocentes* meant children. We find the mental substitution in evidence in Reginold, who wrote *trium iuvenum innocentium necem* in No. 17 and *neci sunt iuvenes innocenti addicti* in No. 20. Then he wrote *tres pueros morti addictos* in No. 36.[54]

This association brought about another liturgical image. The *Benedicite omnia opera,* or Song of Sidrach, Misach, and Abednego, which is the verses 51–90 inserted in Daniel iii in the Septuagint, bears the name of *Laus* (or *Canticum*) *trium puerorum* in the Vulgate and in the *Breviarum Romanum,* even in the reformed version.[55] It is the canticle for Sunday Lauds. That title and the canticle were most popular in Carolingian Ger-

---

[51] Mombritius, p. 302, line 55.
[52] 303.4.
[53] 303.7.
[54] In Otloh's M (No. 28), Cedron says to his wife, "sicut ille liberavit tres illos innocentes de laqueo mortis et de ira constantini imperatoris, ita et filium nostrum nobis incolomen restituat."
[55] Rome, 1853, p. 22.

The Miracle Plays

many.[56] The three in the fiery furnace were a type of the Resurrection. But of more import is that the "three boys" of Daniel became the Old Testament exemplars of scholarship for medieval school boys.[57] Chosen for tutelage in the court of Nabuchodonosor, they exceeded the Babylonian magi in the arts and sciences. Rescued from the furnace by the grace of God through the presence of His angel, they were the Scriptural analogue of the three clerks rescued by Nicholas. I note in Appendix A that the precocious student Walafrid (d. 849) composed his version of the *Canticum trium puerorum* in decasyllabics.

Reginold's *tres pueros morti addictos* may not have been the first occurrence of this substitution; it certainly was not the last. The author who appended the legend of *Getron* to John's *Vita*[58] compared *tres illos innocentes* with the boy Getron;[59] and Otloh, in copying No. 17 into his *Vita* N, gratuitously inserted the word *puerorum: trium* puerorum *innocentum necem.*[60]

Given the connection of schoolboys or clerks with Nicholas, which now appears to have been made in Bavaria *ca.* 1020, when Wolferius and Otloh were studying at Altaich and Hers-

---

[56] Cf. e.g. Alcuin in *Pat. Lat.*, CI, 485 and 468–469; von den Steinen, *op. cit.*, pp. 293–295. Greek fire came to be known as *ignis trium puerorum;* see the recipe given by Bernard Bischoff in *Ehrengabe für Karl Strecker*, 1931, pp. 6–7: "Nam pergentibus Saracenis ad bellum navali certamine in prima fronte navis facta fornace illi insidunt vas eneum his plenum subposito igne, et unus eorum fistula facta aerea ad similitudinem quam rustici squitiatoriam vocant, qua ludunt pueri, in hostem spargunt."

[57] See E. Dümmler, ed., *Das Formelbuch des bischofs Salamo* III, 1857, Ep. xlii, p. 50 (written A.D. 878–882). The letter has been assumed to be the composition of Notker Balbulus (see von den Steinen, *op. cit.*, p. 492). Compare the Prayer of St. Gregory in *Portiforium,* p. 12; also Florus of Lyons in Mon. Germ. Hist., *Poetae* II, p. 529, lines 205–216, and p. 539, lines 44–59.

[58] I have some reasons for believing that these additions were also made in Upper Germany, but I will not discuss them here.

[59] See above, notes to No. 20.

[60] See the illustration in Meisen, p. 332, from a twelfth-century Salzburg manuscript, of three *men* rescued by Nicholas who bear the banner, "Qui tres pueros morti deditos illesos ab..." (from No. 36 above). This medieval confusion has also been often duplicated by recent scholars; Jeanroy, in discussing the hymn *Nicolaus hodie* (*Speculum*, VI [1931], pp. 107–109), says that it refers to *Three Clerks,* as does the hymn *Congaudentes,* though neither, in fact, contains such references. Albrecht, p. 41, uses iconography in stained glass, which shows the three clerks tonsured, as an argument that the fable did not develop from *Stratilates.* But German students, regular or secular, were tonsured in this period.

feld, we can most easily imagine that a story was invented to substantiate the already existing patronage. Or it may well have been that an already existing story, previously unrelated to Nicholas, was adapted to him because of the patronage.[61] Granted the free interchange of legends in hagiography, instances of which I have already noted, it is quite possible that this simple story came either from folklore or from the legendary of some other saint.

As Nicholas' patronage of scholastics spread west, to Hildesheim, to Lorraine (which was then part of the Empire), and on to Normandy with Isembert and Ainard, we find this story catching fire, becoming complicated, and eventually establishing itself as the most popular of all Nicholas legends in the west. At some place along this route, no doubt, the Fleury *Three Clerks* was composed.[62]

---

[61] Baring-Gould (*Lives of the Saints*, 1914, November 11, p. 240) retells from Metaphrastes, *saec*. x (=Halkin [see above, Ch. VII, note 8], No. 1250) a legend of St. Ménas which could have circulated in the west before the year 1000: "A traveller, intending to visit the church of S. Mennas, and make an offering at his tomb, lodged for the night in a tavern. The innkeeper, seeing he had a large portmanteau, murdered the man in the night, cut him up, packed his limbs in a sack, and hung up his head on a beam of the roof, intending to take his money and throw the body into the water at the earliest opportunity. But S. Mennas rode up to the inn door, attended by many saints, put the bits of the man together, restored him to life, gave him his portmanteau, scolded the taverner, and vanished."

[62] Young, *Drama*, II, pp. 330–332. The Hildesheim tradition of dramatizing *Three Daughters* and *Three Clerks* continued. Tibaut of Clairvaux (*saec*. xiii) in a sermon introduces a simile: "Sicut videmus in festo sancti Nicolai quod aliqui repraesentant personam eius ut clericorum aliqui aut puellarum et miracula quae per eum fecit Dominus." (Hauréau in *Notices et Extraits des manuscripts de Bibl. Nat.*, XXXII (1888), p. 327). By that time the plays were widespread.

Coffman (*New Theory*, pp. 72–78) is one of many who treat the St. Catherine Play which arose in Rouen and, according to Matthew Paris, made its way to England (A.D. 1119); his discussion fits easily with the evidence which I have presented. The cult of St. Catherine in the later Middle Age corresponds closely with the cult of St. Nicholas, and I hope elsewhere to point out their common history; see esp. Arnold van Gennap, *Manuel de folklore français contemporain*, I. i (1943), pp. 207–208. They are commonly depicted together in western art. Catherine, like Nicholas, became a patron of scholars, and (in French regions) of adolescent sexuality; they are, for example, the patrons of the University of Paris (Meisen, p. 305). At present I believe that her cult received its greatest western impetus at Rouen with Isembert and Ainard. The Greek monk Simeon's "name lived on at Rouen as the reputed source of important relics of St. Catherine brought from Mount Sinai." (R. W. Southern, *The Making of the Middle Ages*, 1953, p. 54). These relics were the reason for the patronage of Isembert's abbey of St. Catherine. For other evidence of Nicholas-drama in Britain,

The Miracle Plays   113

I have mentioned some connections of Hildesheim and Liège in the time of Notger and then Godehard. They are most clearly to be discerned, no doubt, in architecture which Kurth describes.[63]

The "Einsiedeln fragment" is praised as advancing "beyond the version from Fleury both in variety of action and in characterization."[64] But I think that critics have unnecessarily extended the evidence of the manuscript, which does not specifically indicate a play-script at all. It consists of thirty-six leonine hexameters, which present fifteen speeches. The speakers are indicated only by the content of the lines, though those indications are clear enough. This is classroom eclogue—a dialogue pattern long cultivated assiduously. We note that neither Nicholas nor clerks are mentioned, though the author does deal with *tres ... iuvenes*. Does this text represent a version of the fable which existed before the Bavarian students connected it with Nicholas? Probably not; but there is no evidence to contradict the possibility. Some student, possibly inspired by a word-of-mouth tale, used a portion (or the whole?) to fulfill a class assignment. Leonine hexameters are in the scholastic tradition of *Waltharius*, Rosvitha's epic biographies, and *Ruodlieb*, but not of drama, liturgical or scholastic.

The scholastic quality of the exercise is further indicated by three hexameters which precede it without break and one which follows it without break in the extant manuscript. All state

---

see J. deGhellinck, *L'essor*, 1955, p. 493, and Carleton Brown, "An Early Mention of a St. Nicholas Play in England," in *Royster Memorial Studies*, Chapel Hill, 1931, pp. 62–69. Brown notes in a Cambridge manuscript of the thirteenth century that a "homilist mentions a 'playe' which was to follow after the sermon," the first positive evidence of intrusion into religious service.

Albrecht, p. 115, calls attention that Jacques de Vitry reproaches abbots who aspire to become bishops, *pour jouer au prélat tout comme les enfants qui représentent saint Nicolas dans le récit de ses miracles*. I interpret this passage as evidence that the scholastic tradition continued to be the accepted one and that any later attachment to the liturgy was accidental.

[63] Pp. 326–327.
[64] Young, *Drama*, II. pp. 335–336.

customary scholastic moralia.⁶⁵ Is not the scribe to be followed, who regarded the whole as one piece? In short, I see no cogent reason for considering this text as dramatic composition.⁶⁶

Two themes dramatized at a date later than those of which we are speaking seem especially to belong to the Hildesheim tradition: *The Raising of Lazarus* and *The Conversion of St. Paul*. The earliest dramatic texts for each are contained in the same Fleury playbook that contains the four Nicholas plays. They have been transcribed by Young, among others.⁶⁷ Young says of *Lazarus*: "In its general literary form, and in certain details, the play discloses a learned origin. The very opening rubric *Incipiunt versus* might indicate that the play is a rhetorical exercise from the monastic school. One observes, for example, the didactic and theological, rather than personal and dramatic, touch ..."⁶⁸ He was again presuming that the plays in the playbook were composed at Fleury; indeed, he was later more specific about *Lazarus*: "the anonymous composition written at the monastery of Fleury."⁶⁹ But as Hilarius, disciple of Abelard and Angevin clerk, dramatized the Nicholas *Iconia*, so did he also dramatize the *Lazarus*.⁷⁰ Theological didacticism is not so sustained in the *Conversio S. Pauli*; it appears only indirectly in a speech of Paul enunciating the dogma of the Virgin Birth:

> Cur, Iudei, non resipiscitis?
> Veritati cur contradicitis?
> Cur negatis Mariam virginem
> peperisse Deum et hominem?

---

⁶⁵ *Ibid.*, p. 335, n. 1, and 336, n. 3.

⁶⁶ Indeed, Young, *Drama*, pp. 310–311, injected this possibility into his discussion, though his thought ran in another direction: "As a school-boy [the author] might have been assigned this or that prose legend for versifying." The references which he gave at this point are apropos.

⁶⁷ Lazarus, ed. Young, *Drama* II, pp. 199–208; Paul, *op. cit.*, pp. 219–222. Both have a complex musical score, which Coussemaker, *Drames liturgiques*, 1860, pp. 210–234, gives in full, and Young (*Drama*) in part, by two facsimiles.

⁶⁸ Young, *Drama*, II, pp. 209–210.

⁶⁹ *Ibid.*, p. 211. Young's own accurately descriptive phrase, "didactic and theological," points to cathedral schools.

⁷⁰ Text in Young, *Drama*, II, pp. 212–218.

The Miracle Plays

> Ihesus Christe, Marie filius,
> et Deus est, et homo carneus,
> deitatem a Patre retinens,
> et a matre carnem suscipiens.

But the point at which these two plays are set apart from liturgical plays is in their strophaic structures, which are adaptations of that Hildesheim pair. *Lazarus* is composed entirely in decasyllabic couplets with tetrasyllabic codas; *Conversio* in decasyllabic quatrains without codas. Both have end-rhyme, irregularly two-syllable. These plays, therefore, seem to indicate how scholastic drama moved nearer to liturgical drama. The two traditions tended to become assimilated.[71]

The only other early use of the Hildesheim line in dramatic texts is in the *Sponsus,* which also is the first instance of intrusion of the vernacular into a Latin text. Thereafter, macaronic texts were popular. But *Sponsus* is also notable because its allegorical or abstract cast of agents looks toward development of the morality plays.[72] After an introductory portion in septenarii, all lines, Latin or Romance, are decasyllabic, grouped in quatrains with refrains, except for two penultimate septenarii. The lines are regularly 4 + 6. This decasyllabic verse form, then, starting with the Hildesheim Nicholas plays, seems to have been associated in the minds of authors with scholastic and paraliturgical subjects and presentations. There is no evidence that it was used for dramatic representation inside a sanctuary.[73]

Finally, I wish to accent what I have mentioned before—that the common presumption that this dramaturgy arose in monasteries confuses rather than clarifies the historical picture.[74]

---

[71] Both *Lazarus* and *Conversio* conclude with *Te Deum:* "Et chorus: *Te Deum laudamus.* Sic finiatur." But we have seen that *Te Deum* is evidence only of piety, not of liturgical connection.

[72] Text (with facsimile of manuscript of *saec.* xi/xii from St. Martial, Limoges) in Young, *Drama,* II, pp. 361–364; cf. Grace Frank, *op. cit.,* pp. 58–64.

[73] deGhellinck, *op. cit.,* p. 488, calls attention that in his celebrated description of London, Fitz-Stephen (d. 1191) speaks of *ludi sanctiores* or *repraesentationes miraculorum* (or *passionum martyrum*), which he compares with the ancient Roman theater, *pro spectaculis theatralibus, pro ludis scenicis.*

[74] If this seems overemphasis, see e.g., *Speculum,* XXXVII (1962), p. 139, where Giles Constable quotes Dom Leclercq approvingly: "It seems possible to distinguish from the eighth to the twelfth century in the West something like two Middle Ages," one monastic and the other scholastic.

We are dealing with a German, not a French, development, which occurred in the tenth and eleventh centuries, not the twelfth. German monasticism was less conventual and more intimately linked with diocesan and secular life than was French. The masters taught external scholars as well as oblates. As the tradition continued and moved toward the west, it more naturally gravitated to the cathedral than to the monastic schools. Reginold was a layman until he became bishop. Otloh was a monk, to be sure, as were Godehard and Wolferius before they went to Hildesheim, but they were monks of the German tradition. In Germany reforms of the Cluniac type were only beginning and the religious moved about quite freely in the external world. The legends about the Nicholas *historia* are in one sense highly secular and in another sense pleas against Cluniac rigidity. Isembert was a canon before he became an abbot, and probably Ainard was too. The Fleury which preserved the playbook was, to be sure, the depository of Benedict's corpse; but at the end of the twelfth century it was remote from the days when Odo was abbot of both Fleury and Cluny. Wulfstan was a bishop, and Nicholas of Worcester was the prior of a diocesan school. Nicholas of Myra is developed as the image of the ideal prelate, and there is, to say the least, no attempt to make a monk of him in all the western growth of legends. To find an image of the Nicholas cult and its relationship to the development of secular drama, we have to look to the developing cathedral schools, not the cloisters. Hilarius, the earliest author of a Nicholas play yet to be identified by name, was a disciple of Abelard at Paris; he migrated to the cathedral school at Angers, where he came into an intense Nicholas cult established by the counts Fulk Nerra and Geoffrey Martel.[75] Jean Bodel of Arras (d. 1209/10) was wholly urban, a member of a confrérie and a jongleur.[76]

---

[75] Cf. John B. Fuller, *Hilarii Versus et Ludi*, pp. 11–12.

[76] Edw. Schröder, in *Zeitschrift für d. Alterthum*, XXXVI (1892), p. 239, shows that a scene in the Künzelsauer *Play of Christ's Holy Body*, presented A.D. 1479, was taken from *Three Daughters*.

The Miracle Plays

The variety of uses of anthems and responses, all from the single *historia* composed by Reginold, precludes our attaching the plays to positions in the cursus by means of the references to anthems at the end of scripts.[77] The form of dramaturgy represented by the Nicholas plays owes its development to scholars, and there is no reason to believe that the scripts were ever represented in the sanctuary.

---

[77] As is done, e.g., by Albrecht, p. 110. However, the tendency for drama to creep into liturgy always exists. In the *Aberdeen Breviary*, directions for No. 55 suggest boys' voices for *filiae* and the cantor's voice for *pater*.

CHAPTER IX

Conclusion

BECAUSE THE MAIN ARGUMENTS of this monograph may have been obscured by the presentation of the evidence, I now summarize them.

Shortly before the year 966, Reginold, a secular clerk who had travelled in Byzantium, possibly as a political agent, and who had a reputation for musical skill and for Greek knowledge, composed a *historia*—that is, a series of anthems and responses—honoring St. Nicholas of Myra, to be employed as propers in the hours of prayer, especially the matins. He based his compositions primarily upon the *Life of Nicholas* composed by John the Deacon at Naples about the year 880. Though there is no direct evidence that Reginold borrowed his melodies from any Greek sources, he may have been inspired by the eastern liturgy, for which hymnographers had been composing sanctorals, including musical compositions for Nicholas. Particularly, the image of Nicholas as the morning star, a popular Byzantine metaphor absent from John's *vita* but exploited by Reginold, suggests that Reginold may have used some lost Byzantine compositions, though secondarily.

Although Reginold's *historia* was not the first *historia* in the west, so attractive was it and so in accord with Ottonian imperial policy that it quickly developed a surprisingly active cult. Solely because of this popularity, Reginold was ordained bishop of Eichstätt. He followed up his early success by composing *historiae* for other locally venerated saints. The antagonism of purists and conservatives, who objected to the introduction of uninspired and nonscriptural compositions into the office, was combatted by liberals who invented legends defining the quality of spirituality in the work. To a marked degree, the cult of Nicholas followed the spread of the *historia* through the Latin world. That work can be traced through the Empire, especially

Conclusion

into Lorraine and the Low Countries in the period around the year 1000, when Liège was a center of scholarship of the west.

In Bavaria, its point of origin, the accomplished master Godehard and his disciples cultivated Nicholas as their patron. One disciple, Otloh, composed two *vitae* of Nicholas, one for the abbot of Fulda, possibly when he was resident there, the other for his brothers at St. Emmeram. In the second of these he quoted directly from the *historia*. Clearly, he expected his *vitae* to be used as lections for the office. For both, his content was drawn from John's *vita* and from an unknown *vita* derived from a Byzantine source now represented by Vatican MS *Gr. 821*, essentially a Life of the monk Nicholas of Sion; Otloh used a Latin version whose nearest extant equivalent is Paris, B.N. MS *Lat. 5284*. Otloh's two sources are the sources also of the Austrian and Bavarian Legendaries.

Godehard and his disciple and biographer Wolferius transferred to Hildesheim, where the manuscript which contains the first Nicholas plays and which was the personal property of Godehard was probably written. However, it seems most probable that at least the first play, *Three Daughters,* was composed in Bavaria, at Altaich before Godehard moved north, or at Hersfeld. Directly inspired by Rosvitha's scholastic success in adapting Terence, this Nicholas play is a hymnographical adaptation of her texts to a more masculine subject. The "Hildesheim strophe" in decasyllabics is a popular, or "middle style," equivalent of metrical hymns, composition of which had been the object of scholastic discipline.

Nicholas' patronage of these Bavarian scholars is the earliest evidence of his scholastic patronage. A result was the creation, or adaptation to Nicholas, of the story of the *Three Clerks,* which is the second Hildesheim play. The Einsiedeln manuscript, which is not a play script, may represent this legend cast into the form of a scholastic dialogue of the eclogue type even before the legend was attached to Nicholas' name. All these inventions were developed in or around Liège at the beginning of the eleventh century.

A sudden efflorescence of scholarship and creativity in Normandy centers on a group in Rouen, led by Isembert and Ainard. Both were German, though their province is not certainly known. Both participated in the great development of liturgy of which the *historiae* are primary examples. Isembert may well have been the author of the Prose, *Sospitati,* attached to the Nicholas liturgy. Ainard was composer of the *historia* of St. Catherine. It is probable that the Catherine play that was composed at Rouen and exported to England was closely modeled on the Nicholas plays; it was evidently written by Ainard.

But the *historia* itself first entered England with the Lotharingian scholars who settled in the southwest—at Hereford, Wells, and Exeter. The earliest extant manuscript of the *historia* is Cotton MS *Nero E 1,* copied *ca.* 1060 at Worcester under Wulfstan, prior of the school and later bishop, who intensely cultivated the patronage of Nicholas. From southwest England, the cult rapidly swept the island, so that by the year 1100 Nicholas was venerated by special services in virtually every diocese. However influential the Normans may have been in popularizing the Nicholas cult, they were not the primary agents.

I conclude with a characteristic product of the scholastic cult of Nicholas—a rhythm in rhymed septenarii which, at least in the Aberdeen Rite, was sung by the canons at Compline:

> Cleri patrem et patronum: Nicholaum predicet:
> lete promens votis sonum: clerus et magnificet:
> se cor promptum se cor pronum: sono votis ampliet.
>
> Grecus omnes et Latinus: linguis tribus natio:
> orbis terre maris simul: sexus et condicio:
> hospes civis peregrinus: primi psallat studio.
>
> Semper dedit dat et dabat: cunctis beneficia:
> presul cuius nomen abit: nunquam a memoria:
> quisque mestus germinabit: florens sicut lilia.

Conclusion

Sic in carne constitutus: carnis spernens opera:
nichil agens aut locutus: nisi salutifera:
vinculis carnis absolutus: tandem scandit ethera.

Quod fit virtus caritatis: hoc presenti seculo:
oleum pateat satis: quod manat de tumulo:
et dat munus sanctitatis: imploranti populo.

Sit laus summe trinitati: virtus et victoria:
qui det nobis ut beati Nicholai gaudia
assequemur laureati post vitam in patria.   Amen.[1]

---
[1] The data gathered by Chevalier (*Repert.*, I, p. 203, No. 3399) suggest that these verses were composed in the Loire valley, possibly at Angers. I have copied them from *Breviarium Aberdonense* (repr. London, 1854), vol. II, fos. xii^v–xiii^r.

Appendix A

Decasyllabic Verse of the Hildesheim Plays[1]

THREE DAUGHTERS consists of seventeen strophes of five verses each, four decasyllabics followed by a tetrasyllabic coda. The decasyllabics of each strophe have homoeoteleuton—a one-syllable end-rhyme which in many instances is sound-duplication rather than true rhyme. Meyer's data[2] indicate that this kind of rhyme reached its apogee in the late tenth century, though of course it appeared sporadically in clerical verse as early as the fifth century.

Historians and prosodists have regularly construed this verse form to indicate a French origin of the strophe, though some careful prosodists have been guarded in their assertions. Historians of drama have been less guarded. They have thought it sufficient to refer[3] only to a single assertion of Wilhelm Meyer,[4]

---

[1] I have primarily relied upon the following works:
William Beare, *Latin Verse and European Song*, 1957.
Ph. Aug. Becker, "Die Anfänge der romanischen Verskunst," *Zeitschrift für französiche Sprache und Literatur*, LVI (1932), pp. 257–323; "Vom christlichen Hymnus zum Minnesang," v–viii, *Historisches Jahrbuch*, LII (1932), pp. 145–177.
Michel Burger, *Recherches sur la structure et l'origine des vers romans* (Soc. de Pub. Romanes et Françaises, LIX), 1957.
L. E. Kastner, *History of French Versification*, 1903.
Georges Lote, *Histoire du vers français*, Vol. I, 1949.
Wilhelm Meyer, *Gesammelte Abhandlungen zur mittellateinischen Rhythmik*, Vols. I–III, 1905–1936; other works cited individually.
Dag Norberg, *Introduction à l'étude de la versification latine médiévale* (Acta Univ. Stockholmiensis, Studia Latina V), 1958.
L. Quicherat, *Traité de versification*, 2 éd., 1850.
A. Rochat, "Étude sur la vers décasyllabe," *Jahrbuch für Romanische und Englische Literatur*, XI (1870), pp. 65–93.
H. Suchier, "Die Entstehung des mittellat. und rom. Verssystems," *Romantistisches Jahrbuch*, III (1950), pp. 529–563; *Französische Verslehre auf historischer Grundlage*, Tübingen, 1952; "Die Anfänge des fr. achtsilbigen Verses," *Romanische Forschungen*, LXV (1954), pp. 345–359.
Walter Thomas, *Le décasyllabe roman et sa fortune en Europe* (Travaux et Mémoires de l'Université de Lille, N.S. I, 4), 1904.

[2] Meyer, *Ges. Abh*. I, p. 279: cf. Norberg, pp. 41–43.

[3] E.g., Albrecht, p. 21.

[4] *Fragmenta Burana* (Abhandlungen, Göttingen), Berlin, 1901, p. 118.

Appendix A

though Meyer contributed more relevant discussions elsewhere.[5] In the monograph referred to, he was preoccupied with building a hypothesis of a lost *Zehnsilberspiel* which would account for some facts of *liturgical* drama, in the course of which he remarked: "Die Zehnsilber ist nicht nur in Frankreich geschaffen, sondern auch im Wesentlich dort geblieben... Aber für Deutschland war der Zehnsilber ein ungewohntes Versmass." This remark in that particular context referred only to liturgical dramas, all of which are of the second half of the twelfth century or later.[6] If there was borrowing, the flow would be from secular to liturgical drama. The Hildesheim strophe is, so far as I know, the first of its kind by at least two generations. Young called[7] Meyer's theory "ingenious," but considered it only an "unproved possibility." What Young did not consider, a fact which would have made him even more skeptical, is that Meyer's manuscripts are overwhelmingly German or Italian. Indeed, to Meyer's list Young added other manuscripts, all German.

To attack this fundamental problem in such fashion is not satisfactory. On the antecedents of decasyllabic verse, prosodists have found little to agree about. As Suchier says,[8] "Über den Ursprung dieser Versart besteht keine volle Klarheit." Nevertheless, there is consensus on some points. If we accept that,

---

[5] Granted that Meyer neglected study of the decasyllable, as we shall see, and consequently wrote rather contradictory statements, yet in 1906 he stated (Nachrichten, Göttingen, Heft 2, p. 226): "Denn dazu muss man wenigstens wissen, was das quantitirende Vorbild ist; allein beim Zehnsilber ist das quantitirende Vorbild noch heute strittig... Wahrscheinlich ist das Vorbild des Zehnsilbers die Reihe von 3 1/3 Daktylen: –∪∪ –∪∪ –∪∪ – urbe potens populis locuples; hier also wäre der Sechssilber gleich ∪∪– ∪∪– gesetzt." And he had previously written (*Ges. Abh.* I, pp. 174–175): "Die Zeilen, welche oft einsilbiger Reim oder einsilbige Assonanz bindet, sind meistens in Gruppen zusammengestellt: die trochäischen Fünfzehnsilber in Gruppen von je 2 oder 4 oder besonders von je 3 Zeilen, die Trimeter besonders zu Gruppen von je 5 Zeilen oder, in Nachamung der sapphischen Strophen, zu Gruppen von 3 Zeilen mit einem Fünfsilber, die übrigen Zeilenarten meistens in Gruppen von 2 oder 4 Zeilen."

[6] For Meyer's Zehnsilberstrophe in the liturgical plays, see Eduard Hartl, *Das Drama des Mittelalters,* I, (1937), pp. 39–41, 51; II, pp. 5–8; and texts II, 11 (Prague) 18–19 (Engelburg), 32–43 (Klosterneuburg).

[7] *Drama,* I, p. 677.

[8] *Verslehre,* p. 58.

and look at some indisputable archetypes, we can see that no presumption of French priority is warranted. Indeed, the evidence suggests that the Hildesheim strophe, arising in Germany, was a force—not necessarily primary and certainly not exclusive—in establishing the decasyllabic line as a standard for late medieval and modern rhythm.

The decasyllabic line is one of the most fundamental vernacular verse forms among northern vernaculars; it has given us such lyrics as sonnets, Elizabethan and other drama, and the Miltonic epic.[9] Normally the Italian hendecasyllabic verse of Dante's *De vulgari eloquentia* and *Commedia* is thought to have the same parentage.[10] All French prosodists agree, with a kind of national pride,[11] that the other tongues borrowed it from France or Provence. Although there was not always a consensus among prosodists, all now seem to agree that the verse form developed by heritage or analogy from Latin.[12]

As the name decasyllabic indicates, isosyllabism is essential.[13] Isosyllabism was a basic and conscious principle with versifiers from Augustine to Bede, who, in his text *De arte metrica* explicitly described the principle. But there are many prosodists who believe that accent was equally essential. Among recent writers, Lote has stated the case for isosyllabism alone, Burger[14] for isosyllabism plus accent.

The earliest Romance decasyllabics are eleventh century (*Alexis, Boèce*). These poems and the slightly later *Chanson*

---

[9] "Pendent tout le moyen âge, le décasyllabe, *celeberrimum carmen,* joue un rôle de premier plan, tant en France qu'en Italie" (Burger, p. 20).

[10] Burger, pp. 25–28.

[11] "Le vers décasyllabe (vers de dix syllabes à rime masculine, de onze syllabes à rime féminine) est né sur notre sol" (Quicherat, p. 529). "Le vers décasyllabique apparaît dans l'historie littéraire du moyen-âge tout d'abord sur la terre de France" (Thomas, p. 3). "C'est une opinion courante depuis Diez [1863] que d'attribuer à la France d'honneur d'avoir créé le décasyllabe" (Burger, p. 25).

[12] On theories of the decasyllabic, see Lote, pp. 19, 22; on substitution of syllabism for meter, pp. 12–14. Norberg (p. 190) has summarized: "La poésie latine fut le point de départ de toute la versification romane."

[13] According to Meyer (*Ges. Abh.* I, p. 286), Abelard complained of some ancient (*früheren*) hymns: "Tanta est frequenter inaequalitas syllabarum, ut vix cantici melodiam recipiant, sine qua nullatenus hymnus consistere potest."

[14] See his summary assertion, p. 106. Norberg's view lies rather midway between these two (see chap. vi).

Appendix A

de Roland have verses which are generally but not invariably marked by a caesura after the fourth syllable (4+6), with a tonic accent at each term, and their lines have terminal assonance, which is sometimes rhyme. However, such verses are anticipated by two centuries in the earliest Romance verses (*Eulalie*), which are not regular decasyllabics but are so described in many books of common circulation.[15] The troubadour decasyllabic verses do not appear before *ca.* 1135; there is no instance in the extant poems of William of Poitou,[16] contemporary with *Roland*.[17] Though the troubadours used a 6+4, and that line appears in some later epics (*Girart de Roussilon*), the original line 4+6 remained the popular favorite into modern times. There is a tendency, but no unanimity, to believe that the lyric pattern spread from northern to southern France and that it arose by heritage or analogy from the epic verse.

To approach medieval literary development with the eye centered on these vernacular appearances is an inevitable tendency; but since there is consensus that Latin verse is antecedent, we thereby look through the wrong end of the telescope. In nearly all phases of the study of medieval literature this method has at some point led to egregious misconception. In exasperation, the great Wilhelm Meyer wrote a vigorous protest which has become a *locus classicus* of medieval studies;[18] as a result, subsequent critics have usually been more careful in this respect than were their predecessors of the past century. But even Meyer himself filled in the interstices of his arguments with analogies

---

[15] E.g., Gustave Cohen, *Anthologie de la litt. fr. du M.A.*, 1955, p. 11.

[16] But Suchier thinks otherwise; see Karl Vossler, *Die Dichtungsformen der Romanen*, 1951, p. 92.

[17] "Marcabru e employé dans son poème le décasyllabe de form 4+6 et jamais celui de form 3'+6. Il a d'autre part un vers à césure épique, ce qui indique chez lui une technique du décasyllabe semblable a celle de l'épopée" (Burger, p. 22). However, Norberg (p. 153, n. 1), following Vossler, points to a strophe of *ca.* 1100 which is a close duplicate of the Hildesheim strophe, consisting of 2(4+6)+4:

    Quant li solleiz   converset en leon
        en icel tens   qu'est ortus pliadon,
            per unt matin...

The 4+6 remained overwhelmingly the standard with provencal poets; cf. Meyer, *Ges. Abh.*, I, p. 285, and Burger, p. 24.

[18] *Ges. Abh.*, I, pp. 55–57.

from later literature. In the passage alluded to above, he assumed the French origin of the decasyllabic line, though elsewhere he had denied it. He had not studied the problem directly. His basic survey lists all verse forms known to him from the sixth century, but not a single Latin decasyllabic until the twelfth.[19]

With a *terminus ad quem* for the Hildesheim verses, we need to wipe from our minds all vernacular instances except *Eulalie* as being of definitely later date. If there is a connection with such works as *Alexis* and *Roland*, it is the latter which are derivative.

Recall that culture of about the year 1000 was a projection of the ninth-century Carolingian culture formed by Pippin, Charlemagne, Louis I, and Charles the Bald. Their tradition developed without a serious break along the Rhine and Danube; for the imperial Saxons took up and used what Charles the Fat left them. But no such advances as occurred in Upper Germany in the tenth century were made in France, which was decimated by the Normans in the north and the Saracens around Marseilles. In France an old aristocracy was being replaced by new guerilla leaders drawn from forests and farms. For example, the founders of the houses of Capet and of Anjou are lost in this obscurity; their descendants would become nobles to be honored in the chansons. But in the late ninth and early tenth centuries the arts to glorify them were neglected.

Earlier, in the time of Charlemagne and even of Louis, western Europe had been unified. What especially held it together

---

[19] "Ludus de Antichristo und über die lateinischen Rhythmen," *Ges. Abh.*, I, pp. 136–139. Recently, Lote has pointed to the late eleventh century. In saying that the first 5 + 5 is the Bangor Patrick of *saec.* vii/viii, he continues: "Sauf erreur, le premier exemple qu'on possède en latin du même vers avec coupe quatriéme remonte à 1087, dans le *Chant sur la mort de Guillaume la Conquérant*:

Flete viri	———	lugete proceres;
Resolutus	———	est rex in cineres;
Rex editus	———	de magnis regibus
Rex Guglielmus	———	bello fortissimus ...

Il est donc posterieur a *Saint Alexis*, le premier poème français qui ait été écrit dans ce mètre. Mais personne ne peut supposer un seul instant qu'il en soit une imitation, et c'est bien au contraire, en toute probabilité, *Saint Alexis* qui est la copie d'autres vers latins de dix syllabes césurés 4 + 6 et aujourd'hui perdus." While citing earlier instances, Norberg (p. 153) says, "Ce vers rhythmique de dix syllabes fut, au xiie siècle et plus tard, extrêmement populaire."

Appendix A

was the Latin language, used by the officials of a theocracy, who were simultaneously secular and religious. For them it was a scholastically acquired second language, and the verbal arts based on it were fostered by the schoolmasters. Alcuin was as influential in Reichenau and Salzburg as he was in Auxerre and Tours. In the ninth century, scholars flowed freely from Ireland to Italy. Whatever art developed in a province spread quickly throughout the Carolingian world.

In that world the mark of a scholar and litterateur was his ability to write in meter. *Poetae Carolini Aevi* is stuffed with Latin metrical compositions that have slight justification except to establish the high literacy of their authors. Meter was an art acquired scholastically and indeed archeologically, since the living tradition had been moribund for at least two centuries. This ponderous Carolingian display of metrical verse encourages us to forget that it owed its existence to its rarity. It was a mark of status, and the skill was monumental. If every student that went to school could have easily composed meters, there would have been fewer of them preserved on expensive parchment.

Rhythm occupied a mid-point between harmony and meter. The notion was developed in music, but was easily transferred to purely verbal art. The glosses of Salamo, bishop of Constance and abbot of St. Gall, expressed it simply: "Musice partes sunt tres, id est armonia, rithmica, metrica. armonia est que decernuit in sonis acutum et gravem. rithmica est que requirit incursionem verborum utrum bene sonat an male cohereat. metrica est que mensuram diversorum metrorum probabili ratione cognoscit."[20]

---

[20] Ed. Pietzsch, p. 90. Rhythm is prose, not necessarily significant; meter is verse, necessarily significant. Doubtless the gloss expresses the Carolingian idea gained from Martianus Capella (Pietzsch, p. 75, after Dick's edition of Martianus, p. 499): "Tria tantum mei genera putabantur, mei, id est harmoniae, et est genitivus primitivi. Primum genus est Ydikon: Quae genera formae inveniuntur. Formarum autem tres sunt species, quarum prima in sonis, secunda in numeris, tertia in verbis. Illa autem prima, id est, quae in sonis invenitur, ad harmoniam pertinet; non enim in ea verba aliquid significantia, sed soni tantum sibimetipsis aliqua ratione coniuncti quaeruntur. Secunda autem, quae ad numeros pertinet, nihil alius requirit, nisi tantum convenientem numerum sonorum nihil significantium, aut nihil aut aliquid significantum

Milo of St. Amand (d. 871) apologized for the quality of his verse: if it is not metrical, at least it is rhythmical.[21] Even the Romans before the invasions had lost the ability to distinguish long and short, according to Augustine; he composed his Psalm by simple isosyllabism, *in numeris*. And so the barbarians, four centuries and more removed from Augustine. A Milo composed verse of equal numbers of syllables: if it scanned, well and good; if it didn't, it was still acceptable in the Augustinian pattern. It was rhythm—mediocre verse. A contemporary of Milo wrote:[22]

> Ergo vos cigni lautique decore pavones,
> Cum suavi meatim philomela dulcite carmen
> Et pedibus metricis rithmi contemnite monstra.

This acceptance that rhythm was the poor man's substitute for meter was taught in the one text used in virtually every school, Bede's *De arte metrica:* "Videtur autem rhythmis metris esse consimilis, quae est verborum modulata compositio non metrica ratione sed numero syllabarum ad iudicium aurium examinata, ut sunt carmina vulgarium poetarum ... quem vulgares poetae necesse est rustice, docti faciant docte."[23] The basic principle is

---

absque ullo termino. Tertia vero, quae vocatur metrica, non solum sonos certis temporibus terminatos inquirit, sed etiam cogit, ut aliquid significent, et certum numerum terminumque non excedant: quorum exempla sunt versus et metrum, in quibus duobus certis terminus numerusque pedum ponitur, versui quidem in senario, metro vero in octonario." This concept was related to that expressed by Augustine, *Retractationes* I, 20: "Non aliquo carminis genere id fieri volui, ne me necessitas metrica ad aliqua verba, quae vulgo minus sunt usitata, compelleret." Augustine expresses the learned view *ca.* 400, on which see Norberg, pp. 92–93.

[21] Mon. Germ. Hist., *Poetae* III, p. 674, line 1037; cf. p. 597, lines 418–419. See also Norberg, pp. 92–93.

[22] Paulus Albarus, *Poetae* III, p. 129, line 21. John J. Schlicher, *The Origin of Rhythmical Verse in Late Latin* (Diss. U. of Chicago, 1900), pp. 68–69, first commented on this passage. Albarus, in his *Vita S. Eulogii,* indicated that *ca.* 830 in Mozarabic Spain only "rhythmic verse-composition" was known to the schools: "Nam pueriles contentiones ... epistolatim in invicem egimus et rhythmicis versibus nos laudibus mulcebamus." (*Pat. Lat.* CVX, 708B) Indeed, Eulogius was the first Spaniard of his age to learn metrical art: "Ibi metricos, quos adhuc nesciebant sapientes Hispanias, pedes perfectissime docuit, nobisque ... ostendit." (709C)

[23] *Pat. Lat.* XC, 173–174. *Numero syllabarum* meant *rhythmo syllabarum,* since the student believed that *rhythmus* was an exact synonym in Greek for the Latin *numerus* (see Isidore, *Etymologies* I, xxxix, 3; Martianus Capella ix, 967). I am preparing a new edition of *De arte metrica,* together with Bede's other didactic works, for the *Corpus Christianorum.*

Appendix A

isosyllabism, *numero syllabarum;* but the refinement lies in adjusting it to the ears of the audience, *ad iudicium aurium examinata.*

All we know of the listening Teutonic ear is that it favored a verse broken by a caesura into two hemistichs, each with two stresses. The Carolingian Latin verse in various degrees approaches this Teutonic sensibility.[24] Though the aim of the schools was proficiency in metrics, only the "graduates" attained that exalted height. The others compromised with *rhythmi.* Ekkehard IV of St. Gall (*ca.* 980–1060) described how the boys in school one day displayed their skill before abbot Salomo (890–920). They addressed him in Latin, the seniors in metrical verses, the middlers in rhythms, and the youngsters in prose.[25] Rhythm was the verse form used by the inexperienced, the inexpert, as it was used by the unpretentious middle group; it was an acceptable substitute for perfection.

If we regard only the principle of isosyllabism, we can see no reason why there should be lines of every number of syllables from four to sixteen except ten. Verses of 6, 7, 8, 9, 11, 12, 13, 15, and 16 syllables are at least fairly common in verses surviving from the period. But verses of 7, 8, and 15 were overwhelmingly favored. The reason is found in their tradition. A great many classical models were isosyllabic in structure. The iambic dimeter, 8 syllables, was a rare classical form; but it blossomed into the octosyllabic, the most popular medieval verse.[26] We may judge that Ambrose's taste, reinforced perhaps by Augustine's choice of a 16-syllable line, alone accounts for the popularity of the octosyllabic in the Middle Age. The tro-

---

[24] Scholastic verses which paraphrase Bede's texts *On Times,* in a Mainz manuscript of *ca.* 810 (Vatican, *Pal. Lat. 1448;* see W. M. Lindsay in *Paleographia Latina* IV, pp. 15 ff.), have been edited by C. J. Fordyce, *Bulletin Du Cange,* 1927, pp. 59–73. They ape the Teutonic rhythms of vernacular verse. For the impact of German stress on Carolingian verse, see Norberg, p. 189.

[25] *Casus S. Galli,* 26 (ed. G. Meyer von Kronau, *St. Gallische Geschichtsquellen,* III [1877], p. 105): "Parvuli Latine pro nosse, medii rithmice, caeteri vero metrice."

[26] "Le dimètre, qui est le vers par excellence pendant tout le Moyen Age" (Lote, I, p. 5). I omit discussion of the dactylic hexameter and elegiac as not pertinent to the theme.

chaic septenarius, employed by Hilary and by Fortunatus in his model *Pange lingua,* was invariably 15 syllables, or 8 + 7. Next to the iambic dimeter, this was the most popular tradition. Out of these two, most of the Carolingian rhythms of 7, 8, and 15 emerged.

The third most popular meter with Latin Christians was the sapphic—three verses of 11 with a coda of 5; a fixed caesura in the longer lines divided them into 5 + 6. No one seems quite sure why the sapphic became so extraordinarily popular a model, especially for proper hymns, among the Carolingians. Possibly the marked hemistichs, which gave an opportunity for balanced two-stress, appealed to the Teutonic ear. Alcuin composed pages of sapphics;[27] after Alcuin, they appear less often in Neustria, though their popularity continued further east.

Much less popular, but nevertheless recurrent, was the adonic, a five-syllable line. It tended to fall into pairs, 5 + 5 = 10, with embryonic rhyme, as with Alcuin:

> Te homo laudet,
> Alme Creator,
> Pectore, mente,
> Pacis amore:
> Non modo parva
> Pars quia mundi est.[28]

Alcuin's verse was rather especially revered in Upper Germany, as the incidence of manuscripts shows. The famous *Heriger, Bishop of Mainz,* in the Cambridge manuscript,[29] which is German in subject and presumably in authorship, is a decasyllabic 5 + 5 of adonic ancestry; another in the same manuscript (*Alfrad's Ass*), linked 5 + 5 by rhyme, has its scene laid in the convent of Hohenburg:

---

[27] Cf. *Pat. Lat.,* CI, 556–557, 681–682, 726–727, 1088. See also Norberg, pp. 77–78. Godescalc composed sapphics with reiterated caesural and final rhyme (Mon. Germ. Hist., *Poetae* III, 727).

[28] *Pat. Lat.,* CI, 648. Norberg, pp. 78–79.

[29] Cambridge, Univ. Lib., *Gg. 5. 35,* fos. 432–441; ed. Karl Breul, *The Cambridge Songs,* 1915; Karl Strecker, *Carmina Cantabrigiensia,* 1926.

Appendix A

> Est unus locus   Homburh dictus,
> In quo pascebat   asinam Alfrad,
> Viribus fortem   atque fidelem.[30]

These are scholastic verses, products of the classroom or of alumni of the classroom.

Mention of the Cambridge manuscript, roughly contemporary with the Hildesheim manuscript of Godehard and containing some songs of obviously earlier date of composition, brings to mind the *Modus florum,* generally regarded as coming by direct line of tradition from the Notkerian activity of sequence writing at St. Gall. The first quatrain is decasyllabic with no fixed caesura and no formulated rhyme:

> Mendosam quam cantilenam ago,
> puerulis commendatam dabo,
> quo modulos per mendaces risum
> auditoribus ingentem ferant.

Thereafter the verses are a medley of 6, 8, and 10.

These verses indicate that if isosyllabism is the only essential principle, the Latin schools of any part of Europe could, and did, produce decasyllabics when the spirit moved—that the only reason they were not produced in quantity is that classical and patristic isosyllabic forms, which did not run to ten, were normally the model from which few cared to deviate. But deviate they did. Dom Wilmart traced a metrical decasyllabic of the early ninth century to Aniane.[31] The *Ad Caesarem* of Bruno (of Cologne?) in the tenth century is decasyllabic rhythm with

---

[30] These songs are translated by Howard Mumford Jones in P. S. Allen and Jones, *The Romanesque Lyric,* 1928, Ch. xiv.

[31] *Bulletin Du Cange,* XV (1941), pp. 195 ff. The text appears in Mon. Germ. Hist., *Poetae* VI, pp. 137–140.

[32] *Poetae* V, pp. 377–378. The thirty-two lines begin:
> Scribere qui tibi digna putat,
> Ardua temptat et alta parat.
> At michi, cesar, habunde sat est,
> Si minimum quid ab ore placet.

The editor, Karl Strecker, calls them *Alcmanicum.* I presume that he derived the term from the *Versus metro alcmanico* of Godescalc; Traube's notes, *Poetae,* III, p. 728, cite a number of contemporary verses in this form. Godescalc's verses are divided into assonanced couplets.[32] The metrical adonic yielded a decasyllabic 5 + 5 in the *De Ymno Trium Puerorum*[33] of Walafrid (d. 849), while verses of Eugenius Vulgarius (10th c.),[34] which are decasyllabic 6 + 4, seem to those who hear accent to be modeled on the metrically anapestic catalectic line.

For those who believe only in isosyllabism, a similar *mise en oeuvre* appears to run backward from *Roland* through *Alexis* and *Eulalie* to Prudentius' ballad *Eulalia*.[35] Prudentius composed six five-line strophes, all thirty lines terminating in -*es*. He was fairly successful in maintaining the dactyls of alcmanian, but is uniformly decasyllabic:

> O veneranda dei suboles,
> Inclita patris et effigies,
> Intime splendor et alme dies,
> Qui loca lumine cuncta reples,
> Totus et in genitore manes.

Abbo of St. Germain introduced his *Bella Parisiacae Urbis* with twenty-two "versiculi dactilici" (*Poetae*, IV, pp. 78–79) which are not metrically regular but are regularly decasyllabic. There is no formulated caesura. Strecker indexed them (p. 1162) as dactylic tetrameter catalectic. This *metrum alcmanicum*, apparently quite popular with ninth-century versifiers east of the Vosges, seems to be derived from the Alcmanic strophe of Horace, in which a dactylic hexameter is followed by a tetrameter (*Carm.* I, vii; xxviii; *Ep.* xii), but has developed far toward rhythmic decasyllabic. In Godescalc's verses the rhythm sometimes seems 5 + 5 and is sometimes indiscernible; but the second strophe reads 4 + 6:

> Nempe minus patre nec quid habes,
> Sceptra pari ditione tenes,
> Quaeque cupis, domine, illa potes:
> Nam recreas revocasque homines
> Et patria pietate foves—

[33] *Poetae* II, pp. 394–395. See the numerous instances cited by Norberg, p. 78, n. 5.

[34] *Poetae* IV, p. 424. The *Hymnus de natale innocentum* published among the doubtful compositions of Rabanus Maurus (Mon. Germ. Hist., *Poetae* II, pp. 246–247) consists of ten strophes of five lines (6 + 4) each, without terminal rhyme. The versifier seems to have wanted to compose dactylic tetrameter catalectic: there is some elision and other peculiarities of quantity. But in place of a true quantitative line, he adheres to the formula trisyllable, trisyllable, disyllable, disyllable. Therefore the line reads accentually ′nn/′nn/′n/′n and is rhythmic under any definition.

[35] *Peristephanon iii*, *Hymnus in Honorem Passionis Eulaliae B.M.*, ed. H. J. Thomson (Loeb), *Prudentius*, II, pp. 142–157. The Romance poem *Eulalie* and a Latin *cantica virginis Eulaliae* appear in the St. Amand manuscript, now Valenciennes *143*, copied *ca.* 885. The codex has often been regarded as the personal property of the famous master Hucbald, who was exceptionally informed about music and was closely connected with the schools of Liège and Reims, where he had taught. The codex contains verses in Latin, French, and German. The inclusion of both Teutonic and Romance verses in the same manuscript suggests an origin at Liège, or certainly Lorraine. The Latin verses about Eulalia are not all those of Prudentius; but two lines from Prudentius' poem (164–165) are incorporated verbatim and perfectly fit the decasyllabic 4 + 6. The Romance verses, in assonantal couplets, are in Walloon dialect. The German verses are the famous *Ludwigslied*. My colleague Professor Tubach has called my at-

Appendix A

his paraliturgical song in dactylic tetrameter catalectic, which quite regularly, though not necessarily, yielded a decasyllabic line. Ten Brink, Bartsch, and Gautier thought it natural that the composer of the Romance *Eulalie* should derive his verse form from it.

The isosyllabists would, I believe, regard this evidence as satisfactory to explain the Hildesheim strophe.[36] But for that considerable school of prosodists represented recently by Burger, who believe that accent, whether tonic or stress, was also essential, this answer would not be sufficient. They have engaged themselves to trace a precise metrical progenitor for each medieval verse, including the decasyllabic. For such, there must be

---

tention to two decasyllabic lines (16, 29) among these verses. Although apparently accidental, they indicate that decasyllabic rhythm suited the Lotharingian ear.

Since no other Romance verses exist for comparison from this period, whatever is said about *Eulalie* is bound to be very conjectural. Karl Vossler, *op. cit.*, pp. 167–170, gives the texts and relevant data; cf. Becker, "Minnesang," pp. 172–176. Prudentius' *Eulalia* was composed in strophes of five verses. The earliest imitators were Walafrid and Godescalc, but thereafter the form appeared in France and Italy as well. Decasyllabic verses in quintains rhyming in -a exist in a *saec.* x manuscript from Moissac (*Anal. Hymn.*, II, p. 99). They form a Christmas-table song of happy celebration, which Norberg (p. 130) traces to *Eulalia*. One infers that the 5-line decasyllabic strophe of *Alexis* follows a tradition from Prudentius. Norberg, who cites a number of such decasyllabics (pp. 83–84), calls particular attention to an anonymous hymn (*Anal. Hymn.* LI, p. 134) which he calls Carolingian, in which St. Agatha is celebrated in direct imitation of *Eulalia,* but the strophes are quatrains. It is Norberg's opinion (p. 153) that Prudentius is a possible, but not a certain, model. It seems appropriate here to note aspects of the Alexis cult in the west. The cult started after 977 in Rome. Abp. Sergius and his migrant Greek monks seem responsible for the legend that Alexis was buried *in ecclesia S. Bonifatii*, which thereafter became *et S. Alexis*. To authenticate this development, the Latin *Vita* (*BHL*, No. 286, ed. Acta SS Boll., Iul. IV, pp. 251–253) was composed. Meinwerc, bp. of Paderborn, while in Rome in 1014 with emperor Henry II, saved the army from plague by invoking Alexis (*Acta SS,* p. 244). Consequently he built a monastery for Alexis at Paderborn. The *Vita* is contained in *CLM 14419,* immediately before Otloh's *Life of St. Nicholas* (M). See further H. F. Massmann, *Bibliothek der gesammten deutschen National-Literatur,* IX (1843), pp. 167–171; J. M. Mennier, *La vie de Saint-Alexis* (1933).

[36] J. deGhellinck, *L'essor de la littérature au xiie siècle*, 1955, p. 426, thought it sufficient to say: "L'on n'a pas assez remarqué non plus que ce nombre de sept, huit ou dix syllabes, cher à la versification latine et autre, était aussi la norme de prédilection pour la longeur des incises d'une phrase périodique cadencée, comme le sont entre autres les oeuvres en prose fidéles au *cursus:* affaire d'harmonie pour l'oreille, mais peut-être aussi respect des exigences physiologiques de la respiration." A medieval rhythmist chose the length of the line by what he wanted to say in a line-full; if the strophic form fitted the traditional pattern for his subject and purpose, so much the better.

some demonstrable development of ictus or stress as replacement for long syllables. Burger tries to establish the classical iambic trimeter as the progenitor.[37] But he can present no such persuasive evidence as he and others do when they declare that Ambrose's iambic dimeter begot the octosyllabic.[38] Indeed, despite his addiction to iambic trimeter, his examples of decasyllabic abound in sapphic lines, which are not metrically the same. He tends to disregard the difference, and indicates how these sapphics broke down into medieval rhythms, resulting in the French decasyllabic and the Italian hendecasyllabic; he indicates the accentuation as $4' + 5''$: "Il est d'ailleurs très probable que cette opposition $4' + 5'' / 4' + 5'$ a été favorisée par l'existence du vers saphique, trés populaire durant toute l'epoque mérovingienne. En effet, du fait de la structure, un vers saphique quantitatif, par exemple un vers de Prudence comme Cath. VIII, 1, lu accentuellement, a sans exception un accent sur la quatrième syllabe et un autre sur la dixième.[39] ... la strophe saphique, depuis Eugène de Tolède, pouvait être formée, non de trois trimères iambiques et d'un adonique. Les deux vers devaient donc être considérés comme variantes d'un même metre."[40] For support, he cites the authority of d'Ovidio, who worked on Italian scansion.

But d'Ovidio was not saying the same thing, for he considered the sapphic itself as the legitimate ancestor.[41] In this he was joined by many others; according to Nigra,[42] "L'endecesillabo italiano é nato, molto probilmente, del saffico greco-latino." Briefly, the steps would be first a caesura with feminine ending:

Le emperedre / repaidret en France

and then as the ending became mute, a four-syllable caesura with masculine ending:

Rollanz est pros / et Oliviers est sages.

---
[37] Pp. 107–121.
[38] Pp. 83–87.
[39] P. 112.
[40] P. 116.
[41] Francisco d'Ovidio, *Sull' origine dei versi italiani* ..., Florence, 1897.
[42] In *Romania*, V, p. 430.

Appendix A 135

This was, indeed, the earliest theory of modern prosodists, advanced by Quicherat, Littré, Tobler[43] and many another.[44] But so long as these authorities searched merely to explain the romance verse, and took their instances wholly from the earliest instances of Romance, that is, *Boèce, Alexis,* and *Roland,* and from the verses of Marcabru, their theory was rejected by specialists such as Rochat,[45] Victor Henry,[46] and Walter Thomas,[47] followed by Burger. In the main they assert (1) that there was no warrant for dropping an atone before the caesura, and (2) that the bulk of Romance verse does not follow the theory. They vary in preferring the iambic tetrameter or the dactylic tetrameter[48] as progenitor.

But none of these critics discusses the strophe and the subject.

When we discuss rhythms, not meters, we are dealing with scholastics who knew some theory of classical form, but who could not effectively practice it. They developed a fixed caesura in the Horatian sapphic no doubt in part because the length of the half-lines easily permitted two-stress beats.[49] The introduction of terminal rhyme, growing in popularity in the tenth century, had the effect of forcing the stress onto the final syllable. A one-syllable rhyme has only an incongruous effect if there is a feminine ending. In Latin, if there is any stress at all, it falls

---

[43] E. Littré, *Histoire de la langue française*, I (1886), p. 19; A. Tobler, *Le vers francais ancien et moderne*, 1885, p. 118.

[44] E.g., P. Eickhoff, *Der Ursprung des romanischen-germanischen 11- und 10-silbers (der fünfüssigen Jamben) aus dem v. Horaz in Od. 1–3 eingeführten Worttonbau des Sapphischen Verses*, Wandsbeck, 1895.

[45] "Étude sur le vers décasyllabe dans la poésie française au moyen âge," *Jahrbuch für romanische und englische Literatur*, XI, p. 73.

[46] *Contribution a l'étude des origines du décasyllabe roman*, Paris, 1886, pp. 27–30.

[47] Pp. 26–27.

[48] Fr. Hanssen, *Zur lateinischen und romanischen Metrik*, Valparaiso, 1901, approaches the problem from Iberian verse.

[49] Norberg (p. 189) notes the pressure of Germanic stress on Goliardic verse: "En Allemagne, la forme que prit le vers goliardic vint, sans aucun doute, du fait de la resemblance avec le vers en quatre temps du moyen haut allemand." The prevalent scholastic definition of the sapphic line, as given by Wandalbert of Prüm (*Pat. Lat.* CXXI, 580) supplies a suggestion: "Quinis pedibus, hoc est trochaeo, spondaeo, dactylo, duobus trochaeis decurrit." This unclassical definition might accord with the scholars' habit of making the caesura coincide with the end of a foot and of substituting the two-syllable spondee for the dactyl, with the result that the line would first be viewed as 4 + 7 and then as 4 + 6.

on the antepenult or before, in all but monosyllabic words. It is possible that some cerebral young man, working on as simple principles as did Notker when he invented the sequence-prose, invented a line of 4 + 6 as a reasonable rhythmic substitute for the sapphic 5 + 6. "Le scheme du vers saphique entraînait la chute du dernier accent de chaque hémistiche sur l'avant-dernière syllabe."[50] Furthermore, a Teutonic addiction to the quatrain, which may have been acquired from constant singing of Ambrosian hymns, but which was certainly a mark of later German verse, may have encouraged him to add one more decasyllabic to his strophe.[51] At all events, the coda, now a tetrasyllable on the model of the first hemistich of the decasyllabic lines, seems to me to point in a quite positive way to the sapphic strophe. There is no other obvious model.

Granting the weakness of such a hypothesis, since I can find no confirmatory examples, I am led primarily to place my faith in the parenthood of the sapphic because of the subject matter. In the Church, which in the early Insular and Carolingian periods offered the really stable outlet for the creative urge, the sapphic strophe was not only a favorite, but especially a favorite for proper hymns to saints. One who leafs through *Analecta Hymnica* or the relevant volumes of *Patrologia Latina* cannot fail to be impressed by this tradition. To list the instances would be supererogatory.[52] The Ambrosian octosyllabic, in accord with the conditions of its birth, was especially favored for hymns of doctrine and confutation of heresy. The septenarius for the same

---

[50] Burger, p. 161; cf. Norberg, pp. 96–97. Gevaert, *Mélopée,* p. 81, believed that from *saec.* viii there was a melodic or chant accent uniformly on syllables 1, 4, 6, 8, 10. The 1,4 combination would favor a caesura after 4.

[51] Meyer published a *Canon Evangelorum* with a strophe composed of a quatrain of rhythmic lines 4 + 7 with terminal monorhyme, which he says arose out of Ireland in the seventh century, but which now exists in manuscripts of the Reichenau-St. Gall-Bobbio Irish-German axis. The earliest manuscript is one of *saec.* vii/viii, now at Milan. See "Gildae Oratio Rhythmica, Nachrichten (Göttingen), 1912, pp. 63–67. This is the rhythmic equivalent of the sapphic, but with one more line in each strophe, and no coda. It is therefore one kind of bridge between the metrical sapphic and the Hildesheim strophe.

[52] Nevertheless, note Raban Maur (Mon. Germ. Hist., *Poetae,* II, 252); Walafrid (II, 381, 411, 412, 415(?)); Wandalbert (II, 603); St. Gall MS (IV, 329, 332, 337, 338); Sedulius Scottus (III, 155, 163, 176, 184, 202, 208, 209, 217, 219, 220, 232, 235).

Appendix A 137

reason was favored for processionals and gatherings. But the sapphic was given to hagiography and was close to the heart of the scholarly, who were themselves formulating ideals of Christian living in this world according to their saintly models. Granted that all hymns were *laudes,* praise of God, they had acquired rather specialized traditions. It is not hard for me to imagine a young scholar, as he struggled with his scholastic exercise, evolving the Hildesheim strophe as an adequate rhythmical substitute for the sapphic. Coffman's instinct, it seems to me, was sound when he called the Hildesheim plays hymnographical. But I do not believe that he visualized the difference between the hymnography of scholastic exercise and the composition of those hymns which established their everlasting position in the liturgy of the Church.

In conclusion, I call attention to a few subsequent Latin decasyllabics which seem to have added to a tradition which was in infancy in Godehard's classes. Abelard (master of Hilarius, the author of the *Icon S. Nicolai*) wrote:

> Gaude virgo virginum gloria,
> matrum decus et mater, jubila,
> quae commune sanctorum omnium
> meruisti conferre gaudium.

H. O. Taylor called[53] this line two trochees followed by two dactyls, but all that is indisputable is that it is 4 + 6. A Monte Cassino manuscript of the eleventh century has a hymn to Nicholas in decasyllabic quatrains with one-syllable end-rhyme, but no regular caesura and no coda.[54] No. 42 of the *Carmina Burana:*

> Et aethera   silentio turbavit
> exilio   dum aves relegavit.[55]

The Archpoet:

> Prestet vobis creator Eloy
> caritatis lechitum olei,

---
[53] *Medieval Mind,* II (1914), p. 237. Cf. Norberg, p. 188.
[54] *Anal. Hymn.,* XXII, No. 349, p. 207.
[55] Cf. Meyer, *Ges. Abh.* I, p. 294.

spei vinum, frumentum fidei
et post mortem ad vitam provehi.[56]

John of Garland (Johannes Anglicus, d. 1252), pointing to the *Lament of Oedipus:*

> Diri patris infausta pignora
> ante ortus damnati tempora,
> quia vestra sic jacent corpora,
> mea dolent introrsus pectora.[57]

called it *modus rithmi autenticus ab antiquo tempore.*[58] The Hildesheim strophe with coda appears in a sequence for St. Thomas of Canterbury, *ca.* 1200,[59] and (with one less decasyllabic) in a sequence for St. Martin ascribed to Adam of St. Victor.[60]

Granting, as I think we must, that the extant evidence of Latin decasyllabism is German, and German of a period much earlier than any instances in French (possibly excepting *Eulalie*), then the image of development becomes much clearer. It was in Swabia and environs that most of the experiments leading to modern literature were conducted in the late ninth and the tenth centuries, when large parts of France were reeling under the invasions of Normans in north and west and of Moslems in the south. It is from St. Gall that we have specific testimony about the cult of syllabism. The scholastic generations leading to the composition of the Hildesheim strophe have been traced. In the two decades before and after the year 1000, Liège was the most thriving center of scholarship in Latin Europe, it would seem. It owed its hegemony primarily to the Empire—to the rulers who supported the schools, to its situation upon a primary route from east to west, and to a succession of notable

---

[56] As in Manitius, II, 44, 45; quoted by Jarcho in *Speculum*, III (1928), pp. 536–537.

[57] In 21 quatrains, ed. Du Méril, *Poésies inédites* . . . , 1854, pp. 310–313.

[58] Meyer, *Ges. Abh.* I, p. 301. He listed, pp. 300 ff., many such decasyllabics, but all from *saec.* xii or later, saying: "Vielleicht ist die Zeile 4–u + 6 u– eine freie Erfindung, nachgebildet den alten Zeilen zu 4–u + 7u– und 5–u + 6 u–." As I remarked above, he never really came to grips with the decasyllabic problem.

[59] *Anal. Hymn.*, LV, pp. 357–359.

[60] *Ibid.*, p. 278; cf. pp. 38–39.

Appendix A 139

masters schooled either at Reims and Metz when Gerbert was at his height as a master or else in Upper Germany and Verona. Of these, Notker of Liège (972-1008), who had been provost at St. Gall, is often named as exemplar.[61] These scholars, whose activity seems to have nourished the bloom of diocesan schools in the eleventh century, were in constant communication and interchange with other schools of the Rhine and its tributaries— not only with Reims and Cologne but with Hildesheim, Mainz, and Verona. It was from the Saxon empire that the west drew the scholars of whom Isembert and Ainard in Rouen and Walter and Giso in southwest England are but instances.

---

[61] Emile Lesne, *Les écoles* (Histoire de la proprieté ecclesiastique en France, V), 1940, pp. 341-413, esp. pp. 349-361. Cf. Pietzsch, pp. 110-113.

APPENDIX B

The Music of the St. Nicholas Liturgy

BY

Gilbert Reaney

THE DISCOVERY that the St. Nicholas Office is very probably the work of Reginold of Eichstätt is as important for the musicologist as for the student of liturgy. Like so many unwarranted attributions, the assumption that the work was French and probably written by Isembert, monk of Saint-Ouen, goes back to a casual statement, in this case by Dom Pothier.[1] Dr. Jones has clearly proved that, as Dom Wilmart already saw, the seventeenth-century *Chronicon triplex et unum* was no basis for attributing the complete St. Nicholas Office to Isembert, who may however be the author of the prose *Sospitati dedit*. The main authority for the new attribution to Reginold, the Anonymous Haserensis, an abbot of the diocese of Eichstätt in the eleventh century, was writing only a century after the composition of the office and seems well informed. His detailed account[2] reveals the excellence of Reginold's training, for he was expert in Latin and Greek literature and music. The importance of his composition of the Nicholas office is shown by the fact that he was promoted bishop for it. Even more important perhaps is the reference to the *historica carmina* composed for St. Willibald after the Nicholas office. These reveal that Reginold was undoubtedly one of the most up-to-date musicians of his time, even though we do not possess the actual pieces. Let us examine the evidence carefully, for the clear words of the Anonymous may make it obvious what was considered novel or important in this obscure period of musical composition.

Ornamentation is remarkably varied, and this in the form of *notulas,* doubtless melismas, added at the end of some of the

---
[1] Above, p. 68.
[2] Pp. 69–70.

Appendix B

longest responses. To these melismas Reginold added verses, doubtless what would now be called *prosulae,* since they are said to be in the manner of sequences. The third, sixth, and ninth responses are the ones chosen for this treatment. A further refinement is progressively greater elaboration in the melismas of the respective responses. At least we may assume this, since Reginold added a few verses to the third respond, more to the sixth, and many to the ninth. To cap it all, our musician tried to express the saint's pilgrimage by first having Latin, then Greek, and then Hebrew versicles, and finally Greek and Latin again.

First of all, the importance given to the responses, namely the *responsoria prolixa,* should be noted, since these are musically the most expansive musical forms used in the office and a favorite place for troping. Amalarius discussed one of the most extensive melisma groups in the famous *triplex neuma* of the Christmas respond *Descendit de caelis.*[3] The principle is like that of Reginold, but in *Descendit* the progressive elaboration occurs on each new statement of the response itself. How the different languages were distributed by Reginold is difficult to imagine, though the use of Latin in the third response, Greek in the sixth, and Hebrew in the ninth would fit in best with the pilgrimage. Acquaintance with the Greek language suggests Byzantine influence, and Reginold had in fact traveled in the East.

The widespread use of the Nicholas liturgy in Germany has already been stressed earlier in this book.[4] Dr. Jones suggests that it may have been the earliest one of its kind, perhaps based on Byzantine practices. This could indeed account for its importance in the Middle Ages. The old subjects of offices had been exhausted, and the possibility for new creation inherent

---

[3] P. Wagner, *Einführung in die gregorianische Melodien,* I (3rd ed., 1911), p. 291; music in III (1921), pp. 347 f.

[4] Another reference may not be amiss. The Kremsmünster historian Bernhard Noricus (*saec.* xiii–xiv) says the Nicholas Office was introduced into the liturgy in 1057, and it is indeed among the feasts of the second class in the manuscript *Consuetudines Cremifanenses, ca.* 1100; see A. Kellner, *Musikgeschichte des Stiftes Kremsmünster* (Kassel, 1956), pp. 61 and 28.

in individual saints' lives was responsible for the composition of hundreds of offices of this type. Dr. Jones says that Nicholas office, "unquestionably had precedents enough for its verbal structure...; but its melodies may have been novel."[5] However, Stephen of Liège preceded Reginold by some years, since Stephen died in 920. Mlle. Solange Corbin is of the opinion that only the *Inventio Sancti Stephani* can be attributed to Stephen himself, since there are doubts about the office of the Trinity, and the office of Saint Lambert was simply put together from previously existing metrical pieces.[6] However, although there are metrical pieces in the Lambert office, the majority are rhythmic with rhyme, and the music certainly appears to be new. Peter Wagner thought the office of the Trinity was the prototype of the later offices dedicated to individual saints,[7] though according to Auda[8] the office of Saint Stephen preceded the two others in composition. His reasons are apparently based on the idea of stylistic evolution, for he mentions how the hesitations of the *Inventio* disappear in the Trinity office, in which the poetic form is correctly employed following the rules of metre.[9] Peter Wagner, on the other hand, felt that the Trinity office was less finished in this respect.[10] I am inclined to agree with Auda, though as far as the Nicholas office is concerned, only the *Inventio* seems comparable in date. The other two offices seem later.[11]

At this point it may be well to consider some of the features which Dom Pothier listed as typical of the eleventh-century Norman offices, and which are also important in the cases under consideration here.[12] Needless to say, Dom Pothier considered the Nicholas office as eleventh-century Norman. There can be

---

[5] Above, p. 72.
[6] Above, Ch. V, n. 22.
[7] *Einführung*... I, pp. 305 f.
[8] P. 53.
[9] *Ibid.*
[10] *Einführung*... I, 306.
[11] Cf. the editions in Auda, pp. 58 ff., 113 ff., 187 ff.
[12] "Répons 'Virgo flagellatur'...," *Revue de Chant Grégorien*, V, no. 4 (1896), p. 53.

no doubt that one of the features which distinguishes the newer offices is the gradual abandonment of prose for metre, and one may feel fairly safe in considering this criterion to be of importance in determining relative age. If this is so, the antiquity of the Nicholas office is proved, for Karl Young already showed that there was a predominance of prose texts in this work, verse being restricted to the "proses," which we have already seen are more recent, the response *Magne pater* (No. 56, above) and the antiphons *Decantande* (No. 32) and *Copiose* (No. 57). These three pieces are all in trochaic tetrameter catalectic,[13] which became so popular in the later conductus. In the earliest source, the Nero manuscript, no one of the three is contained in the basic pattern of six antiphons plus four responses for each of the three nocturns, which Reginold would most probably have composed in a block. The three could have been composed later, probably by another author, as the proses were.

Another modern feature of the medieval offices was the presentation of successive antiphons and responses in successive modes, the first antiphon and response in mode 1, the second in mode 2, and so on. This trait, to be found consistently in the offices which Auda attributed to Stephen of Liège, appears in the Nicholas office in a form which may not be fully fledged but is fairly representative of the technique. Both antiphons and responses are arranged through modes 1–8 in perfect order in manuscript S, though in N and W the order of the responses is slightly different, so that for instance *Beatus Nicholaus* (mode 6) follows *Audiens Christi* (mode 4), while in its turn *Beatus Nicholaus* is followed by *Quantam denique* (mode 3) and *Qui cum audissent* (mode 5). The perfection of the order in S may be a later arrangement, but in any case N already has responses 1–4 in correct order, while all the first eight antiphons follow the numerical principle. The last four antiphons of the first group of twelve are all in mode 1, which appears in the office as a whole no fewer than nine times. This further consistency

---
[13] Cf. Young, *Manly,* pp. 261–263.

is to be considered as another indication of modal order. Incidentally, the disorder of manuscript W is probably quite arbitrary. The underlying principle of modal arrangement in the *historiae* is mentioned by Stephen of Liège himself in the dedication to his office of Saint Lambert. Undoubtedly the medieval composer desired a logical correspondence between the number of the mode and that of the lection, which Stephen suggests is related to the proportion one finds in music.[14] The ascetic monk and composer Létalde de Mici indicates another reason for these changes of mode, namely the avoidance of boredom produced by staying in one tonality too long. Reginold in fact has four successive antiphons in the Dorian, which may indicate antiquity. After all, he could have started again with the numerical order from 1 to 4. However, it is clear that consistent modal order in the earlier of the new offices only applies to the first set of antiphons and responses, though it may extend to other groups. Once again, however, the lack of organization in the antiphons and responses for Vespers and Lauds suggests an early date.

The question of transposed modes is interesting. W. H. Frere pointed out that the transposition of mode 6 a fifth higher was equivalent to mode 8 if B flat was consistently employed,[15] and this seems to be the case in both the antiphon *Gloriam mundi* (No. 9) and the response *Beatus Nicholaus* (No. 25). In fact, there is one B natural in the response by way of exception, but this does not seem to me to affect the situation basically. It should be mentioned, however, that an antiphon like *O Christi pietas* (No. 46) in mode 6 untransposed uses the B flat throughout. The music of this antiphon also did service as the antiphon text *O quam suavis* and for the Sanctus of Vatican Mass VIII, to mention only the most important borrowings. The other anti-

---

[14] Mon. Germ. Hist., *Scriptores Rerum Merov.*, VI, p. 387: "Exinde, musicae artis ratione autentica, subnectuntur cum antiphonis responsoria nova, in quibus ordini lectionum respondit series tonorum, quotenus sibi aequando extendi quitur numerus horum."

[15] *Antiphonale Sarisburiense,* Introduction, p. 41.

phon in mode 6 untransposed is *Amicus dei Nicholaus* (No. 41 *alter*): here B is touched only once and the flat is in the clef for this line only.

The composition of Gregorian chant is generally considered today as communal work, so that the part played by individual composers is very difficult to establish. To be sure, this seems to be truer of the earlier chant than of the new-type offices, but from a twentieth-century viewpoint the same principles appear to be in operation. Multiple variations of a series of standard formulas provide the basis for both antiphon and responsory composition, so that the composer's role seems mainly to be that of an adapter or even editor. He will be expert in the combination of different formulas to create a complete composition, and his skill will show itself in the adaptation of new words to existing formulas, which are themselves remolded and elaborated or simplified. In spite of the traditional nature of this type of craftsmanship, it is clear that the new offices made use of a fair amount of new music. Even though this may seem relatively restricted to us, it called forth the remonstrances of conservatives like Létalde de Mici: "The novelty of certain musicians does not please me, for they prefer to be different and disdain to follow the old authors."[16] The question here is: exactly how does this apply to the Nicholas liturgy?

As we have seen, it is the responsories that give scope for new composition, while antiphons, if they are at all novel, are shorter and stick to more traditional formulas. Do the responsories use the traditional formulas? There are two parts to this question. One concerns the response itself, the other the verse which goes with it. Responses, like antiphons, have their own psalm tones according to the mode of composition. A glance at the responses by Reginold reveals that, although he may stick

---

[16] Letald of Micy (*ca.* 1000), *Vita Iuliani*, 4 (Pat. Lat., CXXXVII, 784B = *Acta SS,* Jan. II, 767): "Neque omnino alienari volumus a similitudine veteris cantus, ne barbaram et inexpertam, uti perhibetur, melodiam fingeremus. Non enim mihi placet quorumdam musicorum novitas, qui tanta dissimilitudine utuntur, ut veteres sequi omnino dedignentur auctores."

to the traditional tones at times, for instance in No. 11, *Confessor dei Nicholaus* (with slight variants), he generally prefers to vary them. A completely new psalm tone with no resemblance to the original is not often found, though even in a case like *Confessor dei* it seems common practice to end the verse with the final of the mode. The regular responsory verses in mode 1 end on F, but this is deliberately altered each time by Reginold so as to end on the final. A more typical verse for Reginold is that to *Audiens Christi* (No. 17) in mode 4. It is divided as usual into two parts, of which the first is an ornamented variant of the first half of the usual tone, while the second is quite different, and rather short, ending once again on the final. The variant of the first part is confined to ornamentation of the first note, a central podatus and the penultimate note. The initial punctum a becomes a podatus D–a, the central podatus D–G becomes a torculus D–G–F, while the penultimate punctum a becomes a clivis–virga–podatus–punctum group, a–G–a–G–a–G–G. Here and in other cases there is clear use of verse material in the body of the response itself: in the present example the last 18 notes of the verse occur in the middle of the response. Or is it material from the response which is incorporated into the verse? To judge from *Summe Dei confessor* (No. 36) and *Servus Dei Nicholaus* (No. 55), it is the psalm verse which, even though paraphrased, is the borrowed material. It is clear that the method of varying the responsorial tone, particularly the second half of it, was common practice in Reginold's day, as can be seen in the well-known *Stirps Jesse,* for instance, which probably dates from about the beginning of the eleventh century.[17] It is of course this second half, the new part, which was taken up as probably the best-known Benedicamus melody.

As for the responses themselves, insofar as they do not use verse material, those of Reginold seem to belong to the new

---

[17] Conveniently available with the Corpus Christi text *Comedetis* in *Liber Usualis*, p. 927; with its original text in *Processionale Monasticum*, p. 186.

Appendix B

trend, for they certainly do not employ the standard formulas of the classic type.[18] On the other hand, in spite of their relative elaboration, they do not approach the complexity of *Stirps Jesse*, for example. Although it is probably impossible today to decide what constitute the eastern features, if any, in Reginold's music, the degree of ornamentation may be one of them, and this could have influenced later responses in the same direction. To be sure, we have examples of Gregorian chant which are identical except for ornamentation with Byzantine pieces.[19] But ornamentation is not a prerogative of eastern chant. The problem needs further investigation, taking into account the complete response repertory. The stress on "new" responsories in the choniclers suggests that the melodies are sufficiently different from the old ones to be considered modern, and are, in fact, individual creations. We have even seen that this is true of the more conservative verses, at least in part. The question may, however, still be somewhat bound up with ornamentation. For instance, the verse *Catervatim* of the response *Ex eius tumba* (No. 31) is clearly an ornamented version of the normal first mode responsory tone, except that it ends on the final. The absence of the *tenor* is made up by an ornamented repeat of the *mediatio*. In the responsory itself there are also clear traces of standard melodic formulas, but once again very much disguised by elaborate ornamentation. Example 1 gives the opening period of the respond *Vade Anania* together with that of *Ex eius tumba*. Clearly the

---

[18] See esp. W. H. Frere, Introduction to *Antiphonale Sarisburiense*.

[19] "Ὅτε τῷ σταυρῷ and *O quando in cruce*, for example (music in E. Wellesz, *Eastern Elements in Western Chant*, Boston 1947, pp. 72 f., 99 f.).

Nicholas respond is encrusted with ornament at the side of the other piece. The important drop back to D before attaining a–b flat–a is striking, but perhaps typical of the development technique employed in the newer responsories. In the end, expansion is achieved by a process of ornamentation which almost but not quite obscures the basic formula. On the other hand, a piece like *Beatus Nicholaus* (No. 41) seems completely to abandon previous melodic types, whether in response or verse. Certainly in this case the verse seems to be based on the respond rather than the reverse. The melodic material seems to derive mainly from the opening phrase set to the words *Beatus Nicholaus*. The c–f–c range of the first motif is gradually extended to c–g–c and finally to c–a–c, with the climax on the melisma *oportet* (Example 2), which is the basis for the "prose" *Oportet devota mente*.[20]

The melismas are an interesting phenomenon, though not as long as those found in Ambrosian Chant. They too seem to be part and parcel of the new developments in responsory writing which coincide with the composition of offices for individual saints. The original method was apparently that employed by Reginold in his Office for St. Willibald, namely to apply the melismas to the end of the repeat of the third, sixth, and ninth respond. However, in the form in which it has been preserved, the Nicholas Office has the melismas at the end of every responsory except *Audiens Christi* (No. 17). It is not too easy to be sure of the original order of the pieces in the office, since the order of the earliest sources is monastic, with 12 antiphons and 12 responses, though Dr. Jones feels the office had a secular origin.[21]

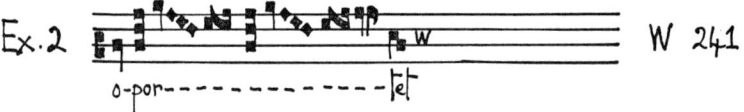

Ex. 2   o-por- - - - - - - - - - - - - -|et   W 241

Even so, I see no reason to suppose that there were only 9 antiphons and 9 responses to begin with. However that may be, the

---

[20] Conveniently available in Frere, p. 358.
[21] See pp. 86–89.

Appendix B

Nicholas Office presents us with some quite developed melismas, usually with the AA or AAB form most frequently to be found. A was apparently sung first by one half, then by the other half of the choir. The longest melismas, e.g., in *Vos qui transituri* and *Descendit,* had several repeats in the pattern AABBA or AABBCC. Of the responds without repeated sections in the Nicholas Office, both *Dum vero* (No. 34) and *Quantam denique* (No. 27) reveal a tendency to repetition. The melisma *sospes* (Example 3), on which the well-known "prose" *Sospitati dedit*[22]

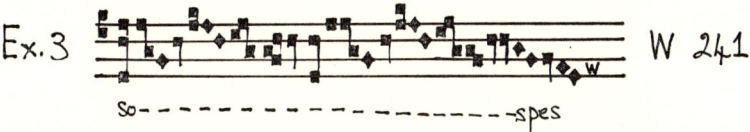

Ex. 3   W 241

So- - - - - - - - - - - - - - - - - - -spes

is only remotely based, has a close melodic resemblance to the melisma *omnem* of the response *Intempestate noctis*.[23] Not merely the opening rise of a seventh broken into a fifth and a third, but also the complete melodic material of the melismas have the same shape, if a different end-result. The most elaborate responsory melismas have some large intervals, though Apel points out that "the combination 5 + 3 upward, outlining a seventh, is not at all uncommon in Roman chant."[24] Much less common is the descending sixth, which however appears in the *Alleluia. V. Multifarie.* In the Nicholas office an ascending sixth opens the melisma of *Confessor Dei Nicholaus* (No. 11), and is repeated a few notes later. The conclusion to be drawn seems to be that the melisma occupies an important part of the Nicholas responses, even if it usually remains of moderate length. Nevertheless, assuming that the melismas originally belonged to the office, they are mature for their time, and a group like the one to the word *sospes* could hardly fail to call forth the addition of "prose" texts. This melisma is particularly remarkable for the amount of movement by leap.

---

[22] In Frere, p. 360.
[23] *Liber Responsorialis*, p. 328.
[24] W. Apel, *Gregorian Chant*, 1958, p. 255.

The antiphons perhaps reveal less freedom than the responses, but nevertheless in the Nicholas Office they are clearly among the most developed works of their kind. A comparison of the melodic types listed by Gevaert[25] shows that the Nicholas antiphons belong with the later ones (Gevaert's third group). For example, I note here a few of the differences between *Stans beata Agnes* (Gevaert's 6T)[26] and *Muneribus datis,* No. 20 (Example 4). The main differences, as usual in the Nicholas Office,

are greater ornamentation. Without leaving the basic formula, *Muneribus* goes up to F on note 2 like *Stans,* a later feature. The B at the top of the initial phrase is not in any of Gevaert's examples. Also a little later c is the high-point in phrase 2, while b flat is the furthest Gevaert's examples go. Phrase 3 is an expansion of phrase 2 and even more elaborate, with a high point on d. Similarly *Pontifices almi* (No. 18) resembles the most elaborate of Gevaert's group 21T, *Lucia virgo*[27] or *Beata Cecilia.* Here again the Nicholas antiphon is more elaborate. The first phrase reaches d and falls back to G, the second gets up to e and drops down to d–c–b–c–d, while the next section attains top g. The compass is wide for mode 7, namely E–g. *Ecclesie sancte* (No. 42) shows its modernity by the drop at the open-

---

[25] F. A. Gevaert, *La mélopée antique dans le chant de l'église latine* (Paris, 1917).
[26] *Liber Usualis,* p. 1341.
[27] *Ibid.,* p. 1324.

Appendix B

ing (DACDD), such as we find also in the Lambert office antiphon *Magna vox*.[28] Clearly this type of antiphon clinging to the bass region and hammering at D and continually returning is modern.

The antiphons to the Magnificat, Invitatory, and Benedictus tended to be more elaborate than the normal antiphons in the new offices; though earlier they were quite syllabic. The popularity of *O Christi pietas* (No. 46) is not surprising, for it is a beautifully formed melody built entirely out of the opening material, the bones of which are the following notes: F–a–c–a–G–F–D–C. The sixth mode itself is outstandingly well characterized in this material and throughout the piece.

The final impression gained from the music of the St. Nicholas Office tends to confirm Dr. Jones' thesis of the date *ca.* 960. In spite of a degree of novelty in both responses and antiphons, their modernity does not reach the extremes of compositions datable in the eleventh century and later. The responsorial tones are not abandoned altogether, melismas are moderately expansive, and actual antiphon and responsory melodies are not so ornate that they bear no resemblance to the standard repertory contemporary with them. Even so, they have sufficient individuality to merit the high esteem in which they were held by contemporaries. A definitive estimate, however, can only be made after the newer offices have been thoroughly investigated.

---
[28] Auda, p. 187.

DATE DUE

DEC 1 2 '79			
MAY 1 7 1988			
3/20/91			
GAYLORD			PRINTED IN U.S.A.